Durgabati Ghose was born in 1905 into a prosperous Bengali family. Her father Girindra Sekhar Basu was the founder of the Indian Psychoanalytical Society. She accompanied her husband on a trip to Europe in 1932, and wrote about her trip in a book title *Paschimjatriki*. A very loving, considerate and liberal woman, she was loved and revered by everyone in the family till her death on 11 January 1992.

Somdatta Mandal is Professor and current Chairperson at the Department of English and Other Modern European Languages, Visva-Bharati, Santiniketan, India. Recipient of several awards and international fellowships, she has published widely both nationally and internationally. She has written two books—*Reflections, Refractions and Rejections: Three American Writers and the Celluloid World* (2002), *Film and Fiction: Word into Image* (2005), and has edited and co-edited twelve volumes of scholarly works including *Indian Travel Narratives* (2010). Her current projects include South Asian Diasporic Cinema and translations of travel narratives from colonial Bengal. She has received an award from Sahitya Akademi for the All India *Indian Literature* Golden Jubilee (1957–2007) Literary Translation Competition in the Fiction category.

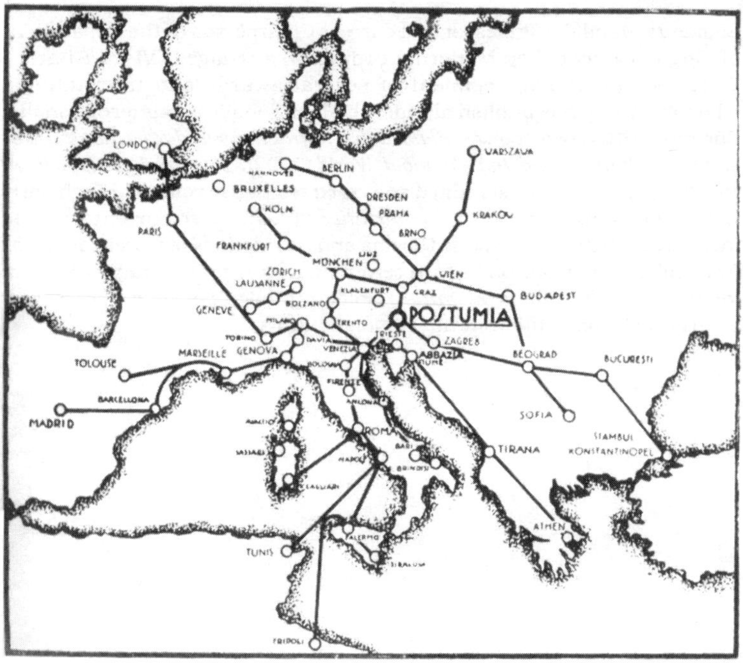

Map of the Europe Tour

The Westward Traveller

DURGABATI GHOSE

Translated from the original Bengali
Paschimjatriki by
SOMDATTA MANDAL

With a Foreword by
ASHIS NANDY

Orient BlackSwan

THE WESTWARD TRAVELLER

ORIENT BLACKSWAN PRIVATE LIMITED

Registered Office
3-6-752 Himayatnagar, Hyderabad 500 029 (A.P.), INDIA
E-mail: centraloffice@orientblackswan.com

Other Offices
Bangalore, Bhopal, Bhubaneshwar, Chennai, Ernakulam, Guwahati, Hyderabad, Jaipur, Kolkata, Lucknow, Mumbai, New Delhi, Patna

First published 2010

ISBN 978-81-250-3991-4

Lasertypeset in Bookman Old Style 10/14
by Eleven Arts, Delhi

Printed in India at
Aegean Offset Printers
Greater Noida

Published by
Orient Blackswan Private Limited
1/24 Asaf Ali Road
New Delhi 110 002
E-mail: delhi@orientblackswan.com

Acknowledgements

Several people deserve thanks. Sri Avijit Sen and Ms Anindita Bhaduri of School of Women's Studies, Jadavpur University, Kolkata, under whose aegis the book saw a new Bengali edition in 2007.

I would like to thank Mr Rajarshi Ghose and Mr Sudeepto Ghose, grand-nephews of Durgabati Ghose and copyright holders of the original Bengali book for granting the necessary permission for translation.

I am grateful to my friend Purabi Panwar who took the trouble to read through the manuscript and suggest changes wherever needed.

This book is dedicated to my father, Late Ganapati Das who instilled a love of travel in all of us and my mother Swarnalata Das who told us many stories of her visit to England in 1952 but never penned them down.

The Empire Thinks Back
A Foreword

Ashis Nandy

In 2004, in a literary conference at Hyderabad, I first heard of Durgabati Ghose's travelogue on Europe, *Paschimjatriki.* I had strayed into a panel discussion where Somdatta Mandal was speaking on travel literature produced in India during colonial times. Her fascinating paper included a section on the writings of Bengali women on Europe. One of these women was Durgabati Ghose neé Bose who visited Europe in the autumn of 1932 and published her book soon after.

As it happened, I had worked some years earlier on Girindra Sekhar Bose, the first non-western psychoanalyst, and Durgabati was his daughter. Like many Bengali psychologists I could claim an especial relationship with her father. I never met him but had to face him in my teachers and in the works of earlier generations of Indian psychoanalysts. I was also a fan of Girindra Sekhar's brother Raj Sekhar, better known as Parashuram—an eminent writer, translator, lexicographer and social critic—and often wondered about the intriguing complementarities between the two siblings. I had reasons to be curious about Durgabati's book. Later, Amit Ranjan Basu, who had done some excellent work on Girindra Sekhar, gifted me a copy of *Paschimjatriki* and I remember the enthusiasm with which I read it.

Somdatta may disagree, but it was pretty obvious to me after reading *Paschimjatriki* that Durgabati's reaction to Europe was in many ways typical of urban, middle-class, educated Bengali women, willing to abide by the conventions of such travel writing. She was waiting to be pleasantly surprised by her encounter with Europe, for the Europe she chose to encounter was the Europe her class and her community had already paradoxically internalised. The elements of delectable shock and surprise of discovery were built into the design. In many sections of colonial India, particularly the *bhadralok* of Calcutta, when it came to Europe, you were expected to surprise and shock your compatriots, and yourself, in unsurprising ways.

Understandably, Somdatta's article grants that there was already a tacit comparative frame within which Europe was fitted in such travel literature. Europe made sense as India's antonym and, to a sizeable section of India's urban, educated middle-class, India too had begun to make sense as an antonym of Europe. After all, had not the new breed of theories of progress claimed that India lived out Europe's past, while Europe was a slideshow of India's future?

Flouting geography, at the centre of that imagined Europe was England, surrounded by France, Germany, Italy and perhaps, Greece as the original source of European modernity. The rest were the other Europe, complete with touches of the fearsome and the exotic, acquired from Edwardian popular literature circulating in colonial India—from Bram Stoker to Arthur Conan Doyle—and from tourist guides and popular travelogues. On one side was Transylvania, Moravia and Bohemia, on the other, Paris, Rome and Berlin. The Europe I am talking about was mostly a mix of the experiences and dreams of generations of eager Indian students going to Britain for higher studies and sometimes wandering off to the Continent out of curiosity or a sense of adventure. Occasionally the mix was spiced by the touches of the romantic and the heroic, thanks to stories circulating of dreamy, expatriate Indian revolutionaries secretly training or conspiring to topple the British Empire with the connivance of European powers. Everyone in India's modernising middle-class 'knew' Europe—even the ones who had never been to Europe and never read about it seriously. Naturally when they talked or wrote about Europe, it made more sense to Indians than to Europeans. In any case, it was the high noon of imperialism and few Europeans cared what Asians and Africans wrote about Europe.

Durgabati's Europe, too, had to be mainly a backdrop for her conversations with her Bengali readers. The romance of Europe she carried within her and communicated to her readers in a slightly out-of-breath tone in *Paschimjatriki*, was partly a discourse on India and partly a respectful, *sotto voce* argument with the Europe within the cultural frame of India for the sake of Indians. If *Paschimjatriki* sought to infect them with a sense of adventure, it was an adventure that came with controlled risk—a bit like the staple suspense in regular crime thrillers in which, despite all the secret conspiracies and hidden evil, the darkness and the shadows, the readers usually know how the story will pan out or, at least, how the hero and the villain will fare.

Also, the way Durgabati recounts her adventures in Europe make them variations on familiar Bengali domesticity, interpersonal patterns and femininity played out outside their natural locale. This gives the travelogue a stamp of predictability or familiarity and, at the same time, a touch of robust, irreverent charm and self-confidence. The oscillation between the two captivated me in Hyderabad when Somdatta read out her brief description of Durgabati's meeting with Sigmund Freud, her father's hero, friend and training analyst separated by three thousand miles. Freud has an important place in my intellectual firmament and any Indian's face-to-face encounter with him could not but be a matter of deep curiosity for me.

Durgabati had dutifully carried with her a letter of introduction her father had written to Freud. She had read about Freud in newspapers and journals and had heard about him from her father, his colleagues and friends. It seems she had to make some effort to find Freud in Vienna, despite his iconic status. She did not know German and was uncomfortable even with English. In addition, Freud's home did not have a nameplate. But when she located him and met him in an autumn afternoon in 1932, she felt let down. She had expected him to be 'very impressive', perhaps because she had imagined him to be a variation on the more imperious, English men she had met or seen in Calcutta, then still the capital of British India. Instead, he turned out to be a 'simple, ordinary looking old man' holding a burning cigar in his hand and having teeth 'all framed in gold'. (One wonders if Durgabati had ever seen and was influenced by the imaginary portrait of Sigmund Freud that her father and the Indian Psychoanalytic Society had commissioned and then gifted it to Freud on his birthday in 1922. The noted artist Jatindra Kumar Sen, remembered for his drawings for Raj Sekhar Bose's famous short stories, did the painting. It is said that Freud, on seeing it, had remarked that it made him look very English.)

Freud, of course, was very happy to meet his friend's daughter and after 'exchanging pleasantries', they went out into the garden. Durgabati says,

> After that we came back and sat in the room. Two huge furry dogs ran in. One jumped into his lap and the other

put up his two feet on my lap and tried to climb up. I was stiff with fear. I did not have the habit of living with dogs but kept quiet due to courtesy. Picking up an ivory statue of Lord Vishnu from his table, he said, 'Your father had once sent this to me.'

Suddenly the dog gave a loud bark and jumped upon my lap. Forgetting everything and pushing him out of my lap, I stood up from the chair. Dogs in these countries were used to getting hugs from visitors, so why would he listen to me? Considering me a spoilsport, he started barking louder. The professor understood my situation and he quickly locked the two dogs in one room. They kept on barking loudly and banging the door.

'Are you afraid of dogs?' he asked me.

'Yes, I don't have dogs. I am very scared of them.'

'Why are you afraid?' he asked further. 'I myself feed the dogs by making them sit on my lap. Your father treats other people's mental diseases. Does he know about your fear of dogs?'

'Yes, of course he knows,' I added. 'He himself does not have any dog.'

The professor was really surprised to hear this.

That was the moment when Durgabati almost entered history and also probably cleared the way for Somdatta to do so. For Durgabati concludes the story by remembering that she kept thinking in her mind that if she could speak English well, she 'would have asked Professor Freud what his own love of dogs signified. As a famous psychologist, what had he to say about that?'

The revolutionary healer and thinker—equipped with a concept of dissent in which an enlightened vanguard courageously fights not only for a new concept of human nature and a new technology of demystification but also for the redemptive possibilities of a new mode of self-confrontation—missed the chance of listening to his lay critic from Calcutta. For Durgabati never spoke out. The first psychoanalyst was left with only his passing encounter with a friend's daughter whose father had avoided his analytic responsibility of interpreting her fears to her. She must have remained for Freud merely a fleeting presence—a complex-ridden daughter of an esteemed colleague, representing uncritical everydayness and dull domesticity. Durgabati's ordinariness, diffidence and the coordinates of her geopolitical location had doomed her dissent.

Somdatta in her work emphasises on not only the diversity of travel literature in colonial times but also gingerly touches upon some of the running themes in them. She tells us that the diversity comes mainly from the amount of empirical details in the narratives, the unifying theme from the assumption that a travelogue must convey information. She scarcely notices that her lively analysis of middle-class, modernising Bengali women's response to Europe is neatly summed up in an apparently timid, self-depreciating comment that could have come from an ironic counter-discourse or from an interpretation of interpretation. The Empire may or may not have talked or written back through Durgabati, but it may have found in her one analysis and to analyse back on its behalf.

Durgabati says that she was held back by her inadequate English. Does that mark out the outlines of another subplot? She was after all well-educated and lived in the capital of British India. Is she trying to say or has she somehow sensed that the metropolis has a language and that language refuses to be yours in crucial moments? Instead of giving you voice, it silences you? Are such inarticulate, defiant silences lost forever? Or do they survive, as in this instance, in the interstices of a vernacular text as the fading memory of a generation that had the gift to fight but not the authoritative language of dissent?

Somdatta Mandal now brings Durgabati's complete travelogue to the English-speaking world. Perhaps in the hope that, eight decades after the event, a new generation of readers may be more adventurous and grant Durgabati's story more dignity and look beyond her domesticity, predictability and modest silences to explore the intimations of extra-ordinariness that undergirded her everydayness. If they decide to do so, they will be beholden to Somdatta for rediscovering Durgabati Ghose as a person having her own mind, in full control of her critical faculties.

Translator's Introduction

The last three decades of the nineteenth century and the first few of the twentieth witnessed an explosion of travel literature from Eastern India, particularly from Bengal. That Calcutta was the capital of British India till 1911 was of course, one of its reasons. The spread of English education for the middle-class in the nineteenth century played a significant role in developing such narratives. It is through learning English that the enlightened Bengali of the new age learnt to see modern Europe. Also the emancipation of women, inculcated to a great extent by the progressive Brahmo Samaj movement, made the weaker sex venture into Victorian homes. Apart from the opening of the Suez Canal in 1869, these sea voyages to Europe and to England in particular (often referred to by a general term 'Vilayet' in most of the writings) gained greater impetus and were recorded in a variety of literary forms ranging from diaries, religious tracts, personal memoirs, plain literary texts and even poetry.

During the nineteenth century the Hindu pundits had prohibited foreign travel. For any Hindu during those times, crossing the *kala pani* or the dark waters of the oceans and visiting Europe was not only a cause of turmoil in personal life but was equivalent to a social revolution. For many such adventurers, return resulted in social ostracism or committing religious penance—*prayaschitta.* That the onrush of travel to the west persisted in spite of such hazards at home, speaks of the coexistence of conservatism and emancipation in the social history of Bengal.

Unlike their male counterparts, living in an era that still primarily assigned them the role of the angel of the house, middle-class Bengali women hardly travelled to the west alone. Barring a few exceptions, most of them went along with their family members, usually accompanying their husbands, fathers or sons. The kind of experiences they relate, and the metaphysical roads they travelled were often quite different. For most of them, the very act of travel bore the signature of modernity. Their narratives crossed boundaries of genre and purpose—personal documents by ordinary women who organised their texts and mapped the self according to the journey, geographic movement providing the root metaphor by which they made sense of their lives.

Krishnabhabini Das, who visited England in 1882 and wrote the first full-length travel narrative called *England-e Bongo Mohila* [A Bengali Lady in England] (1885) was of course not the first one to transcend the boundaries of the home and the world. Before her, the two Dutt sisters, Aru and Toru had traveled in Europe from 1869 to 1873 with their father Govin Chunder Dutt. Indira Debi Chowdhurani in her book *Puratani* gives us some information about Rabindranath Tagore's sister-in-law, Gyanadanandini Debi's experiences in England in 1879. Even Rajkumari Bandyopadhyay had successfully travelled to Europe during this period. In *The Autobiography of a Princess* (1921), Suniti Devee, hailing from the royal family of Coochbehar, describes in great detail several of her visits to England. Interestingly, apart from Saratrenu Devi's *Parashye Bongo Romoni* (1916) [A Bengali Lady in Persia], Sarala Debi Chowdhurani's *Burma Jatra*

[Trip to Burma] and Hariprabha Takeda's *Bongomohilar Japan Jatra* (1915)[A Bengali Lady's Trip to Japan], none of these women travellers wrote any full-length travelogues on their experiences in the west—to Europe and England in particular.

In this respect, Durgabati Ghose's *Paschimjatriki* [The Westward Traveller] published in 1936, offers a significant contribution to the history of women's travel narratives from colonial Bengal. Her narrative follows Krishnabhabini Das's work exactly fifty years later and the difference between the two works are quite significant. The shift from the nineteenth century to the twentieth as well as the different purposes of the two visits along with the class difference of the two narrators make the texts very different in form and content.

For most of these middle-class women writing professionally for publication was never the prime motive. They wrote for themselves or their family, publication being only an incidental concern. The women travellers to Europe worked to shape their feminised personae characterised by conventionality, conservatism, and domesticity even as they imitated a male-dominated tradition of travel and travel writing. But provided with new knowledge about people and places, they recorded what they encountered in an almost ethnographic fashion. Thus their narratives typically explored an individual woman's expanding consciousness as she moves into previously unknown areas of the world. Her experiences, recorded often for her own later reflection, often reveal a growing sense of place in both what is called 'home' and in the world at large. This binary perspective of juxtaposing the 'self' with the 'other' ultimately helped in creating a new form of 'self' in these writers. A new land intensifies their connection to the mores of their own cultures, and these mores are often either reconsidered or rejected as the writer experiences other ways of being.

BIOGRAPHY

Born at a time when the birth of a girl child was hardly considered to be significant enough for official recording, the exact year of Durgabati's birth is still under speculation. It is tentatively around 1905/1906.[1] She was the eldest child of Girindra Sekhar and Indumati Basu of 14, Parsi Bagan Lane in North Calcutta. The Basu family was quite well known for the patriarch Chandra Sekhar Basu, who was a Sanskrit scholar of repute. He had married three times and had four sons (Sashi Sekhar, Raj Sekhar, Krishna Sekhar, and Girindra Sekhar) and five daughters (Indumati, Kumudbati, Ushabati, Lilabati and Hiranyabati). Though not very rich, the family's upper middle-class affluence came from education that ranged from literature to scriptures, from science to psychology.

At the time of her birth, Durgabati's father had just enrolled for his studies at the Medical College. Growing up in this academic ambience, Durgabati read many other kinds of books apart from her school texts. In 1917 when Girindra Sekhar received his Masters degree in Psychology, Durgabati was about twelve years old. After completing her schooling from Brahmo Balika Sikshalaya, in 1921 she got married to Rabindra Chandra Ghose, son of Sir Charuchandra Ghose of Bhowanipur in South Calcutta. The very same year her father, Girindra Sekhar Bose received his DSc degree from the University of Calcutta for his dissertation on 'The Concept of Repression' and became well-known as a

[1] In his book *The Savage Freud* (New Delhi: Oxford University Press, 1995), Ashis Nandy mentions it as 1908. According to Durgabati Ghose's nephew-in-law, Tarun Kumar Ghose, this is incorrect. According to Amit Ranjan Basu, it is unlikely that she graduated from Brahmo Balika School and got married at the age of 13. See Introduction to *Paschimjatriki* (Kolkata: Dey's Publishing House, 2007, p. 25).

psychologist. In 1922 he founded the Indian Psychoanalytical Society.

Like many other women of her times, Durgabati's intellectual stimulation received greater impetus in her in-law's house. The family was quite westernised for the times. Many male members of this family had travelled to Europe with their wives. Rabindra Chandra's grandfather, Debendra Chandra Ghose was well-known in Calcutta for his political and social work. His son Charu Chandra was bar-at-law, became Chief Justice, and later received knighthood. Charu Chandra's eldest son Rabindra Chandra studied at Presidency College and was also bar-at-law, though he did not gain as much reputation as his father. He was more interested in looking after the ancestral property and found interest in social and cultural activities rather than practicing law. He encouraged Durgabati in all her activities, especially in writing and travelling. Rabindra Chandra and Durgabati did not have any children.

Durgabati occupied a special position in her in-law's house. Blending both eastern and western values, she was unconventional in many ways. It is said that during festivities she would decorate the house with neem leaves instead of the traditional mango leaves; unlike most Bengali women of her times, she wore a gent's watch and covered shoes. Her literary activities ranged from writing poems to handwritten volumes of children's literature that she would gift to various children living in her joint family. A very loving, considerate and liberal woman, she was loved and revered by everyone in the family till her death on 11 January 1992.

THE TRAVELOGUE

Durgabati's sojourn to Europe lasted for about four months—130 days to be exact. In the travelogue, the specific dates of the journey from June to September are mentioned but not the year. From family sources it is known to be in the year 1932. Though she accompanied her husband, his name or his profession does not feature in the narrative. Only on one occasion she casually mentions that her husband was once a student in England. We do not even get to know the exact reason for her travel. It might have been for mere tourism or for medical treatment. Moving across Europe in an affluent manner with Thomas Cook and Company arranging the itinerary, Ghose's experiences are quite different from other fellow Bengali women travellers.

Like many other travelogues of the time, the quality of narration is not uniform throughout this work. Sometimes there are too many boring details about the journey itself, more emphasis being given to the context rather than the text. Following a somewhat set pattern, there are a lot of details on the voyage and the traveller. This was because the sea voyages that took these travellers followed more or less the same route. They boarded a ship in Bombay and then went via Aden, Port Said, Suez Canal, the Red Sea, till they reached some port in Italy or France. Then they took the train through Switzerland and Austria to reach Calais. A steamer across the English Channel would land them at Dover or any other English port. So the first phase of Durgabati's narrative also tells us about sea-sickness, monotony of travel, observation of different co-passengers etc. though a lot of her feelings were filtered through her upper middle-class upbringing and perceptions.

The next important approach is cartography—emphasising on a sense of place, space and landscape. Like most Bengali travel narratives we get descriptions of voyages out and voyages in, where the starting and destination points of journeys are physical places. There is an aesthetic appreciation of the landscape and Durgabati speaks of the places they visited in such a manner that the reader will be able to savour the exotic but unaffordable horizons of the west through accurate details. Thus there is a lot of touristy kind of information—actual names of places within the cities, the streets, the museums, the transport system, the ports, the hotels, the parks, actual train rides etc. Though it does not read like a travel guide, her narration is full of interaction with ordinary people, be they fellow travellers or hotel owners or beggars. Focusing on accurate description of the 'real world,' she is always concerned with verisimilitude.

One interesting fact about this travelogue is that even within its set pattern, it also offers what I term, nuggets of history. The long sections in Italy during Mussolini's time when air raid evacuation was practised at different hours of the day; the humorous personal interaction with her father's friend, Professor Sigmund Freud in Vienna and other incidents offer fodder for historians of subaltern studies. Another interesting aspect is the manner in which Durgabati thought of and spoke in binaries—juxtaposing the dichotomy of East and West, Third and First World. Reading accounts of her travel lets us participate in acts of intercultural perception, ethnography and cultural construction in processes of understanding and misunderstanding. Further, we can evaluate the situation in relation of the self to the world. Fluctuating between the poles of subjective experience and objectivity, the author often takes recourse to comparative analyses.

Examples of intercultural encounter, often arising from not knowing the language, and making value judgments can be cited at random. For example, during the initial phase of wonder, Durgabati is enamoured of the ways in which the British police performed their duties; the systematic movement of the London underground. While travelling in the streets she realised that compared to men, women travellers were much more in number. She even noticed the beggars on the streets, the poor children pestering them for pennies near the Thames underground station; but the day she notices an English woman wiping her child's dirty face with spit, her utopia about Vilayet is totally shattered.

The last but most important aspect of the travelogue is its depiction of the female gaze. The genre of women's travel writing tends to contain slightly different features, such as apologies for what women travellers claim to be the amateurish nature of their work and justification for why they travelled at all. While women travellers tended, like men, to uphold the values of empire, they also sought to enjoy the escape from life at home. But what they narrated was usually related to detailed descriptions of customs, religious practices, habitat and dress codes they encountered in their travels. Though her travel was undertaken under considerable affluence, like the typical Bengali middle-class woman, Durgabati's narrative is also filled with many minute observations that are missing from men's travelogues. For example, on a visit to the Regent Park Zoo, she notices that lettuce and salt were being given to the lions and tigers along with their raw meat. 'Like the sahibs, probably the tigers were used to having salads for their meals,' she wryly comments. On another instance, her keen sense of observation is noticed when she tells us about two huge signboards on the streets of London. One showed the head of a cow, below which was written—'Home-killed! Come and buy a few pieces.' She even identifies a funny advertisement for Indian curry powder that shows a native Odiya cook squatting on the floor and grinding masalas on the stone. So when did cultural stereotyping begin, one might ask. Actually such minute details save the narrative from its other run-of-the-mill counterparts.

Durgabati's narrative was first serialised in the Bengali monthly *Probashi* in seven installments in 1935–36 (Ashwin to Chaitra 1942). Along with 32 pictures, it was published in book form as *Paschimjatriki* in Ashwin of 1343 (October 1936) by Ranjan Publishing House, 25/2 Mohanbagan Row, Calcutta with a price of Rupees 2 & 12 annas. The author Durgabati Ghose had the title 'Sreemati' prefixed to her name, making it quite clear about her middle-class bhadralok cultural identity.

In January 2007, School of Womens' Studies, Jadavpur University and Dey's Publishing House, Kolkata jointly published a new edition of the book. Edited by Avijit Sen and Anindita Bhaduri this scholarly work contains a detailed introduction by Amit Ranjan Basu, the editor of the unpublished selected works of Girindra Sekhar Basu. Two reviews of the book, one by Sri Mohitlal Majumdar, published in *Probashi* (Magh 1343; Jan–Feb 1937) and the other by Sri Chanchal Chattopadhyay in *Parichay* (Baisakh 1344; April–May 1937) add to the scholarly merit of a relatively lesser known woman writer. The picture of Durgabati and her husband and a sample page of her handwriting add weight to the anonymity of the writer. The editors have also painstakingly added in the appendix a comparative study of the spellings and changes between the serialised version and the 1936 edition of the book. Interestingly, the prefix 'Sreemati' to her name has been dropped in this edition. Durgabati went to England for the second time twenty-five years later. She did not write any travelogue on this trip but simply wrote a long unpublished poem called 'Bilati Samachar' ['News from Britain'] which has been included in the 2007 edition.

Before concluding, I want to mention a few things about this translation. About five years ago, I had casually picked up the dust-laden volume of *Paschimjatriki* from the shelves of our University Central Library when I was writing a research paper on travels to the West from colonial Bengal. I had neither heard of the writer, nor of the book. What interested me, however, was that it was published in the same year as Jyotirmala Devi's *Bilet Deshta Matir* (Calcutta: Gurudas Chattopadhyay & Sons, 1936), another travelogue by a Bengali woman. Since then, along with other travelogues, I began translating certain interesting sections and then ultimately the whole book. This translation—a labour of love—done during breaks in academic commitments, forms part of an intended series of translations of Bengali travelogues to the West that I hope will offer new perspectives to the occidental gaze. Since for a long time the hybridity of travel writing meant it was not taken seriously, it is time we considered the relative aesthetic appreciation of this genre. Also, at a time when postcolonial studies emphasise retrieval of archival material, and the boundary between literature and history blurs, I hope this humble effort will add a new dimension to the greater debates on centre-margin binaries and transculturation.

31 March 2009 Somdatta Mandal

S One

On the afternoon of 11th of June, paying obeisance to all the elders and seeking farewell from all our relatives, with tears in our eyes we boarded the train at Howrah Station. We, meaning my husband and myself. The long journey ahead had unconsciously created an anxiety in our minds. But that did not last long. As the train started, the lure of distant lands made us feel light-hearted.

12th of June, 1932. We are on our way to Bilaspur. It is six in the morning. There was no difficulty at night. The train is shaking too much, so can't write properly. There is no water in the tap. Washing my mouth with water taken from the pitcher, drinking some more water, I am waiting for the water supply to resume. With my hair tied in a knot, I'll take my bath as soon as there is water in the tap.

Yesterday afternoon at Kharagpur Station I had bought two big Malda mangoes that resembled medium-sized *kharbujas*. Costing six annas a pair, I did not know how they would taste. The train is stopping frequently in the middle of fields; may be the track is not in proper order. This whole day also passed off in the same manner. During the day when the train was passing through Madhya Pradesh it was very difficult to while away time. The heat and the dust are terrible, so I am sitting with a wet towel over my face. It cooled down a little in the evening and we went to sleep after dinner.

Around nine the next morning, 13th of June, the train arrived at the Victoria Terminus Station in Bombay. Our relative Sri Nirendranath Ghosh and our friend Mr Somji came in two separate cars to receive us. Both of them wanted us to go to their respective houses and freshen up before leaving for the dock. It was ultimately decided that we would bathe at Sri Nagendranath Ghosh's house, have lunch at Mr Somji's place and then proceed to the ship via the office of Thomas Cook from where we would collect our tickets and make other necessary arrangements. We left our heavy luggage at the station itself in the custody of a Thomas Cook employee. Later when we went to the dock, we were totally surprised. The whole place was filled with people—innumerable number of passengers along with an equal number of friends and relatives. Everyone was bidding farewell to each other. Most of the women had tears in their eyes. To be honest, my mood was also not very upbeat and so I sat on one side with a glum face. The passengers were divided into two groups—men on one side, women on the other. Two doctors, one male and one female, were seated in two separate enclosures and they were just cursorily feeling everyone's pulse for a few seconds. They asked a lot of questions and verified our names from the printed list of passengers kept on the table. The passengers stood in front of the huge ship on Ballard Pier that was occasionally letting out sirens so loud that one felt the blood curling in one's stomach. A long ladder hung from the top of the ship at the base of which stood stern-looking sergeant of huge build. He allowed people to climb only after checking their papers. At the top of the stairs was another person doing the same thing. The porters of Thomas Cook & Company had already loaded a part of our luggage, so we climbed up with the rest. Our friends also bought separate visitors' passes to see the interior of the ship. An employee of the ship accompanied us to our cabin, numbered 161 and 162. I started checking my luggage in this temporarily hired room. The furniture consisted of two immovable beds fixed on the floor. There was a huge chest of drawers for storing clothes, a table, a small tea table, a wardrobe with a mirror fixed on it, a couch with cushions and a small waste paper basket. Two small cabinets for storing chamber pots inside them were placed on either side of the beds. On top of it was a water jug along with a glass.

The Motto Nave Victoria

There was no fan inside the cabin so it felt intolerably hot. Cold air blew in from two pot-like vessels hung from the ceiling above each bed. There was only one porthole and the cabin boy shut that down too, gesticulating before my face to tell me, 'No open.' The poor fellow was an Italian who could not speak good English. Oh! I've forgotten to mention that our ship was called *M. V. Victoria* in English and *Motto Nave Victoria* in Italian. It did not run on steam but had an engine like a motorboat. The ship left the dock at around one o'clock in the afternoon. Within ten or fifteen minutes, the Bombay High Court, the top of the Taj Mahal Hotel, the church, the houses, the people—all blurred and mixed together with the blue water all around us. Friends who kept on waving their handkerchiefs from the Ballard Pier became indistinguishable; only the kerchiefs could be seen from the distance, as if a flock of white pigeons were flying. The ship was swaying quite a lot. Its interior seemed like a big decorated hotel floating on the water. And just then the bell rang for lunch. On arriving at the dining hall I was astonished to find it a huge place where about two hundred different kinds of people were having their meals together. At the front and back of the hall were two very shiny wooden frames on which were fixed brass figures of human beings, plants and deer. A band was playing in front and I liked its Italian tune. The food was very good—but one cannot possibly have all the different items served. While eating, it seemed as if someone was constantly trying to push me off from my chair. I understood that the sea had started disturbing us.

The dining hall had a cooling system so we did not feel the heat outside but when we went to the deck after lunch, the sea breeze was hot and carried a fishy smell. I thought of walking around the deck for a while but my head started reeling. Feeling disgusted, I went to the drawing room and sat on a comfortable chair. The steward brought a cup of coffee but left after I told him that I did not need it. Before leaving, he turned back twice to observe me carefully. I felt even more disgusted; what was it? Was I an elephant or a horse? Why did he have to stare at me? I was already suffering. A little later he arrived with a plate of lemon and ice cubes and left it in front of me. Moving the curtains and opening the windows wide enough to let in fresh air, he instructed me to put the ice cubes in my mouth. I then realised that he had noticed my giddiness. These men were very efficient in such cases of seasickness. Feeling uneasy even while sitting, I hit upon the bright idea of seeing around the whole ship at this opportune moment. At least my mind would be diverted and I would feel less giddy. Putting an ice cube in my mouth I strode down the staircase to the first floor but oh my God! It seemed as if an earthquake had begun. Gathering courage, I asked a steward to show me the way to the third class. Climbing down a flight of stairs and ascending another, I reached the third class deck. I did not have to go far. Thrusting myself into a deck chair right in front of me, I started vomiting. All the food that I had had for lunch were out. A little later I observed that everyone around me was in a similar state. Holding a glass of water in one hand and a towel in the other, everybody had pulled up their chairs next to the drains at the edge of the deck. Pungent odour of vomit filled the whole place and the ship's labourers were constantly washing it clean. Realising that the situation was not very favourable, we decided to return to our own cabin. Holding the stewards' hands we toddled along to lie down straight on our cabin beds. Pressing a bell next to our bed a steward and a stewardess came in and helped us to change our clothes and wash our faces.

My head started reeling as soon as I tried to lift my head from the pillow. Lying down I kept watching the shadows of the waves flickering on the highly polished wooden beams and heard water lashing outside on the closed porthole glass. I now understood why the steward had told me 'No open.' Our cabin was on the third floor, and the water level was rising above that. The bed was sometimes tilting at such angles that it seemed I would fall down. The ship was rocking in all directions. There was no air in the cabin and both of us were incapable of getting up from our beds. Using a stick and the handle of an umbrella, we tried to adjust the overhead air vents. I tried to imagine the comforts of my own house and at the same time comforted myself with the thought that unless we endured a little suffering, we would not be able to see so many new places. All the passengers of the ship were in the same situation. Two and a half days passed like this.

Before boarding the ship, our friend Mr Somji had given us some good Alphonso mangoes. So, for the next two days we survived on them and lemon juice.

Today is the 16th of June. The condition of the sea is a little better. Somehow managing to tidy myself up, I took the lift to the deck. Sitting with closed eyes on a deck chair and discussing with other passengers how they endured the ordeal of the past two days, I am feeling better. We are crossing the Arabian Sea; the colour of the water is like blue-black ink. The breaking of the waves makes the white surf seem as if someone was scattering white cotton wool all around us. This wild beauty made my head reel further. As the day advanced, the colour of the water grew darker. Today the portholes in the cabin were all open. I heard that we would reach the port of Aden around midnight and leave again at eight o'clock in the morning.

Today is the 17th of June. It is quarter past two in the afternoon and I am writing this just after lunch. The ship

The Water Reservoir in Aden

had reached Aden around three o'clock at night and had again departed around seven this morning. I did not venture to go on land as I was not feeling physically fit. We are now crossing the Red Sea. On one side we have Africa, on the other side we can see the distant shores of Arabia. Moving constantly westwards, the ship's clock was adjusted by putting it back by half an hour each day. We were told that the temperatures would rise as there was desert on either side of our route. The colour of the water is now pale blue, and I don't know when it will turn red.

Our friend Sri Abaninath Mitra and his wife are also travelling in this ship. The third class here is known as the second economic class. Since he did not suffer from any seasickness, Abani *babu* not only relished and digested all his meals but also regretted not being able to eat more. 'Since they have taken the full fare, I should realise it as much as possible', he stated. People from different nationalities were travelling in their section of the ship. He had acquainted himself with most of them, enjoying their company, as well as entertaining them. Today at Aden, he brought a tin of pineapples and presented it to me. I in return gave him some flattened rice, mango jelly and spices that my mother had given me before departure. He also gave me a bottle of mango pickle, but I did not take it to the dining hall fearing that I will have to share it with others. Abani babu had tutored the Italian cook in their section to prepare Bengali *aloo dum* and it really helps other passengers if there are a few more people like him. There is no foppery in the second economic zone, hence the people there had spread out large mattresses on the floor and were busy playing cards, chess, etc. One passenger was practising simple tunes on a box harmonium. Since their rooms did not have any portholes and were extremely stuffy, they spent most of the time on the deck.

I really liked the camaraderie among the passengers, especially the way one looked after the other when sick. The Italian men and women were quite good looking. The people who played music during dinner and served food were all handsome. They spoke English in ways small English boys do—pronouncing potato without the word 't'. One day they served me 'potato in jacket'. Today I have ordered rice and mutton curry for lunch but do not know whether the Italian cook will be able to make it.

After crossing the Suez Canal, we are planning to disembark at Egypt to see the pyramids. Let's see what happens. The passengers of the ship have formed themselves into various groups. This morning I went to the kitchen to see how bread was made. The dough was being made into different shapes like sea fish, crabs, snails, shells etc. which were then quickly patted and baked in electric ovens. My head is still fuzzy, but gradually I must explore the ship further. It is now six in the evening and the drill to evacuate a sinking ship has just been completed. The ship's siren blew exactly at five o' clock; all the passengers rushed to the deck and put on their life belts. Suppressing his smile, the captain inspected whether everyone had fastened the belts properly, as if there was a great impending danger. A few minutes later, the siren went off again, everyone unfastened their belts and left smiling.

There are many other amusing things to observe in the ship. Every night, after dinner we are shown films. We watch a movie everyday. After leaving Aden, we can see sand dunes within the sea—the sunlight reflecting on them making them resemble icebergs. At night we observe lighthouses over these small hills and moonlight reflected on the water. But in spite of such beautiful sights, I sometimes feel morose with the immensity of having only water all around us.

21st June. Within the last two days we arranged separate tickets sold in the ship for visiting Cairo. All letters to be sent to India had been deposited in the ship's post office by the 19th of June. Thomas Cook took care of all the facilities for the passengers. We were supposed to go to Cairo once the ship entered the Suez Canal. So after dinner and the

Map of the Suez Canal

film show, we retired to our cabin instructing the cabin boy to wake us up when the ship entered the Suez Canal. He informed us that the ship had nearly reached it. Thus, abandoning the idea of taking a nap, we hurriedly packed a small suitcase with essential things—a change of clothes, two small towels, a small tin of condiments, a cake of soap, a small bottle of iodine, a few ear buds, a bottle of hair lotion, one bottle of chrolodoc, hair brush, comb, etc. Wearing our woollen coats and with umbrellas in our hands, like many other people we also kept waiting on the chairs in front of the post office.

The post office offered money exchange facilities so we took some Egyptian currency too. A little later we could see the lights of the city of Suez. As the sound of water and the lashing of the waves reduced, from the edge of the railing it seemed that the ship had reached the mouth of a wide river. A huge wooden plank was floating under the ship and an electric lamp focused on it. A ladder was lowered down over that plank. There was moonlight everywhere. Below we heard a motor launch with people's voices in a riotous commotion—shouting, bargaining and quarrelling in Arabic. All the Cairo-bound passengers climbed down the steps and got into the launch. It was ten past one at night there; the time in Calcutta would be quarter to four in the morning. In his hoarse voice and broken English the Arabian boatman announced that on reaching Cairo we should not trust anyone except the guide because the whole city was full of swindlers. Since Thomas Cook had organised our trip, they were supposed to look after us. The motorboat quickly took us to the Suez harbour where four or five Buicks were already waiting. We split into groups and boarded the cars. In our car there were three Bengalis, two American ladies and the driver—a total of six people. The car first took us to the Suez customs office where they searched our luggage to ascertain what kind of tourists we were. Then they checked our passports and let us go. Most of the communication was through gestures because people here spoke only French and Arabic and very little English. Our car then ran at full speed. In the clear moonlight one could see the cold wind creating shifting patterns on the sand like waves on the ocean. This was a section of the Sahara desert that we were crossing.

People here did not call it Sahara; they called it the Nubean Desert. In the moonlight the small cactus shrubs dotting the sand resembled newly growing hair over a clean shaven head. There was no other tree in sight. The weather was strange, the cold air and fine sand hitting our faces like ant bites. On the way a tyre of our car burst suddenly and we had to wait for half an hour for it to be replaced before resuming our drive. I do not remember exactly how many miles we drove, may be nearly eighty or so, before we reached Cairo, the capital of Egypt. We stopped at the Savoy Continental Hotel where Thomas Cook had arranged our meals. As soon as we alighted from the car, a short, stout, reddish looking man came and introduced himself as our guide. He wore long white and loose pajamas, a brown open collared coat and on his head was a red fez cap with thick black tassels. Another man, whose features were completely different, and who was also a guide, accompanied him. He was well-built, dark, wore loose white pants, a long green robe, with curled *nagra* shoes on his feet. While one of them told us everything about pyramids and mosques, the other would give us different information. We observed both of them quite well. After washing ourselves in separate sections meant for ladies and gents, we sat down to eat. The tea arrived without the toast and the toast without the butter, leaving us hungry. One of our fellow passengers went in to enquire about the state of affairs and came back with the information that the servants had just woken up and were still disoriented. Anyhow, in due time, we did receive everything—tea, bread, eggs, porridge etc., following which we went back to our car.

After travelling for some more time we reached the base of a pyramid. The coldness of the night had disappeared altogether and it was very hot and sunny. A group of camels was waiting for us and while everyone else climbed up on their back, only Mrs Kashinath and I decided to ride a strange-looking horse-drawn carriage. On our way the two horses blessed us with a lot of jerks and jolts! Sand was blowing all around us. The pyramids of Egypt are one of the seven wonders of the world! I was surprised to see the huge columns on either side of the entrance as well as the canopy above them. There were no joints in the stones. Each piece was made out of a separate mass of stone and each of them was as huge as a room. The guide informed us that during those days there were no cranes to lift the stones and the slaves did all the work. I looked around and kept wondering at the number of slaves who would have been required to construct it and the strength that would have been demanded of them.

A lot of photographers were wandering around us. Once ordered, they would take our pictures and deliver them to us later. A funny thing happened when we were taking the photographs. Though we refused to climb up on the camel's back, the guide insisted that we should do it at least once to take the picture. We tried to explain that we loved to take pictures standing on the ground but he was adamant. He stated that if we did not climb up on the camel's back, at least we should hold the reins and stand next to our husbands for it would be a good pose. Reluctantly I tried to do so once but just at that moment the camel let out a strange cry and I left the reins and decided not to be so

The Pyramids in Cairo (Durgabati Ghose standing on the extreme right)

adventurous. After all, I was a Bengali woman used to getting up in the morning and concentrating on dutifully carrying out my household chores—beginning my day in the kitchen. That such a person had seen the pyramid with her own eyes was more than enough. I had to look after all the pleasures and comforts of my husband and so it was not necessary to hold the reins of his camel. The museum was closed because it was a Monday and so we could not see any Egyptian mummies. The tomb of Tutenkhamen also had to be excluded because if we had to see it, we would have had to travel to far away Luxor to do so.

২ Two

From the pyramids we went to the banks of the River Nile. I do not know about other people but to me the river seemed like the Maniktola Canal in Kolkata. Though there was not much water in the river now, we were told that it was more beautiful when it was in full spate. After that we returned to our hotel. Our heads reeled in the heat so merely washing our hands and feet was not enough. I summoned a tall boy, and like a mute expressing herself in sign language, I tried to ask him for some water to bathe. However, his reply was unintelligible, so I had to find out other means.

The person whom Thomas Cook had employed to take care of us understood French, Arabic and English. We conveyed our heart's desire to him and he promised to make the necessary arrangements. Since his company would not provide it, he told us that we would have to pay five shillings extra per head. Our contract only allowed us to wash our hands and feet in the basin, he confided. Due to the tremendous heat, we agreed to what he said. So a dark servant took us upstairs to a bathroom that had both hot and cold water. He even provided us with one big and two small towels. Putting a few drops of clorodoc in the water we relished our bath, changed our clothes and came downstairs for lunch. Hunger made us enjoy our lunch—chicken pish-pash, soup and a few pieces of sweet, red watermelons. We were longing for some ice cream and on expressing our desire were immediately served some.

After lunch we went to visit the Cairo bazaar. The roads, literally narrow lanes, were lined with innumerable shops on both sides and these were crowded with men and women.

The women were all dressed in black. They were wearing different kinds of clothes but the black covering was a must. Half of their foreheads and the area from below the nose to the lips were also covered. From the part of their faces that was visible, I realised that they were quite beautiful. There were fruit stalls, shops selling silk materials, gold, silver, bronze and copper ornaments, utensils and vegetables. While on the streets, we could feel the heat of the blazing sun overhead; a hawker with a basket full of wares shouted out from the streets exactly in the manner they do in our country. Most of the houses on both sides of the street had their doors and windows tightly shut, probably due to the heat.

Camels on the streets of Cairo

Camel-drawn carts with wooden frames filled with huge black watermelons were moving along the streets. The drivers, along with a few small children, were walking beside the carts and enjoying bites from half a watermelon. A dead body on its way to the grave passed our car. The coffin was decorated with different designs of flowers, leaves, human figures and horses. Passing all this, we reached the

Mohammed Ali Mosque. On our return journey, we saw a poor Egyptian woman waiting with a jug of water on her shoulders. She gestured that we could pay money and drink water if we were thirsty. If the car halted on the street, photographers and peddlers selling beads, picture postcards etc. would immediately surround us. There was also a group of hawkers selling small, live green insects known as Egyptian scarabs. From ancient times the Egyptians would bury the dead bodies of their relatives along with these poisonous insects with the belief that if any pilferer came to loot the ornaments in the grave, they would be bitten by these insects. Thus they acted as guardians of the dead. We have come far from those times and such beliefs. No one uses these insects any more while burying the dead. And yet the hawkers still try to sell them to foreign tourists. We were told that they did not have so much poison now. When they came to sell these insects to us, I told them that we have plenty of them in our own country and did not need any more. We heard that some crazy American tourists still bought these insects, took them back home, fed them, and stored them in display boxes in their drawing room to show them to their guests. The women even killed and framed them in gold, turning them into lockets to wear on their chains. What strange desires people have! The people in Miss Mayo's country have really strange tastes.

After travelling the whole day, we came back to the hotel for some time. The train that would take us to Port Said was still some hours away. The sleepless night, the long car ride and travelling the whole day had exhausted us so much that we all started to doze off in the chairs. A little while later the guide came and informed us that the car arranged to take us to the railway station had arrived. The photograph taken in front of the pyramid also arrived by then. The foreign women started discussing their hairstyles in the photograph—

The Mohammed Ali Mosque in Cairo

how 'sweet' someone's smile was. Each of us had bought a copy of the photograph.

We had to wait for some more time at the station for the train to arrive. Then another journey began. At around eight at night we had our dinner in the restaurant car of the train. The sun was just setting behind the date palms. After dinner, all of us took a nap. On reaching Port Said, cars brought us once again to the seashore where our ship *Victoria* was already waiting for us. The whole ship was dazzling with electric lights. It was about eleven o' clock at night and after the exhausting day the sight of the ship gave us much pleasure as if we had returned to our own home. Dinner was over by then and everyone was busy dancing. We were very hungry but nothing was available except drinks.

On entering the cabin we found that our beds were ready with extra blankets—probably it would be cold at night. After a nice warm bath, we had some mango jelly brought from home, thoughtfully packed by mother, a glass of water, and went off to sleep. The steward's knock woke us up in the morning. With a smile on his face and a cheery 'good

Port Said

morning' he asked us whether we would have breakfast. It was already nine o' clock. We got up very reluctantly and asked him to serve it in the room itself.

22nd June. We are feeling quite fit and well. It is gradually turning cold. The cabin is very comfortable now and we are just passing below the Italian boot. The ship will halt at the port of Naples for two hours tomorrow and we will try to see the city during that time. But however much we travel abroad, I keep on missing my own home, especially during meals and bedtime.

23rd June. Early in the morning, as the ship moved closer to Naples, I looked out from the porthole of our cabin. Bits of paper, string, rags, and empty tins were floating on the water. A few boats with fresh white sails sped past us. At a distance, the famous volcano Vesuvius stood with its huge body—white and dark black smoke emerging constantly from it and melting in the sky. After a quick breakfast, we prepared ourselves to disembark. As soon as the ship reached the dock, the same kind of ladder was fixed again and after showing our passports to the police, we came down. Thomas Cook had arranged a covered taxi and four of us—my husband and me, Sir Joseph and Lady Bhore climbed into it. Our friend Sri Abaninath Mitra and his wife disembarked at Naples because they had made prior arrangements to visit other countries from here.

While driving along we saw something like stone walls on either side of the road. They resembled black granite slabs from which roads were later cut out. The driver explained that it was lava that had emerged from Vesuvius. We first visited a coral factory where different kinds of corals collected from the seabed were cut and polished into necklaces, earrings, bracelets, photo frames, etc. They were good to look at. Then we went to the city of Pompeii, which once upon a time was a rich, thriving and beautiful place,

A street in Pompeii

but had been all of a sudden turned to ashes in a single day by earthquake and fire. Houses, men and women, animals, shops etc. had got buried under the molten lava. Now, a few artifacts were excavated and displayed in museums. These included beautiful houses, shops, stone dolls, pictures, chairs, tables, surgical instruments, test-tubes, gas jars, water decanters, earthen utensils, pottery, burnt ropes, onions, walnuts, and even whole eggs. It took us about two hours to look around Pompeii. Having taken a walk to explore the city made our feet ache.

The city of Naples, located on hillsides next to the sea, is beautiful. Trams, buses, motorcars and cycles were running there. The hill slopes were full of vineyards, apple and cherry trees and different kinds of flowers. We came back to our ship and proceeded towards Genoa. Our ship reached Genoa on the morning of the 24th of June. All the passengers had to alight here along with their luggage as the ship would halt for seven days and then go back to Bombay. As soon as

Naples—A Glimpse

the ship stopped here we found people all around conversing in Italian. No one knew English but they understood French. Whenever we wanted to speak they would ask, 'Parlez-vous francais?' meaning 'Can you speak French?'

Dr Kalidas Nag had written and instructed a Bengali man to come and meet us. Approaching us he introduced himself, 'I am Kalidas babu's student, studying here. My name is Birendra Chandra Singha. Please come with me.' Seeing someone from our own country made us heave a sigh with relief.

Mr A. Firpo, partner of Firpo Company at Chowringhee in Calcutta, had come to see Italian lakes at that time. We were acquainted with Mr A. Firpo and his younger brother came to receive us on his behalf. One of his brothers, Professor Enricho Firpo lived in Genoa. He did not know English but his wife did; so he brought along his wife to converse with us properly. They requested us more than once to stay there for two days but since we had already planned to leave for Milan that very day, we refused their offer. Mrs Enricho Firpo had danced somewhere for the whole night and needed rest. So she returned home. Professor Enricho Firpo invited Sri Birendra Chandra Singha along with me and my husband for lunch. Because of his influential position we did not have to open our baggage for checking. First we went to the railway station and deposited our luggage in the cloak room. After that we visited the office of Lloyd Stristino to verify whether berths had been reserved for our return journey, but unfortunately we could not get the necessary information. The London office of Thomas Cook might give us further information later. Professor Firpo went to his office for a short while. It was decided that we would travel around the city of Genoa along with Birendra Chandra Singha for some time and then meet him at his office for lunch. As we walked along the streets, people kept staring at this strange sari-clad lady. The women were even more curious and some of them even started following us, making me feel rather uneasy.

Small black mosaic tiles with floral motifs were inlaid in the footpath. On our way we saw flower vendors selling different coloured flowers in large baskets that resembled huge upturned cane seats. The dress of the flower-seller was equally colourful and one felt like standing and admiring her beauty, her structure and her posture. On either side of the streets there were three-storey high magnolia glandiflora trees in full bloom and they had made the entire area fragrant. Buses and trams plied down the undulated roads on the hill slopes. We went to Sri Birendra's house where he lived as a boarder. There all the ladies flocked together to see me; some admired my sari, others my bangles, and even the dot of *sindoor* on my forehead. A little later we went to Professor Enricho's office and he took us to a big hotel called 'Siramare.' After lunch we rested there for a while and then came to the station where beautiful paintings adorned the pillars on the wall. It was around three-thirty in the afternoon when we boarded the train to Milan with our luggage. Birendra Singha told us that on reaching Milan if we needed coolies, we must call out saying, 'Facino!' Professor Enricho consented saying, 'Si, si, si', meaning 'Yes, yes ... that's correct.' As he knew Italian quite well, Birendra acted as the interpreter for all of us. We left for Milan at 4 p.m.

As the train moved, we kept watching the beautiful scenery on both sides. Sometimes we even saw blue lakes. On reaching Milan at 6 p.m. the shout for a 'facino' immediately brought in four or five porters. They helped us board a private motor bus that would take us to our destination. The name of the hotel where we were supposed to stay was written on the bus and two men were standing next to it. One came forward and said, 'We belong to the hotel and have come here to pick up foreign tourists. The hotel is about ten or fifteen minutes away. You take your luggage and go in this bus and then send it back for collecting other tourists.'

These people spoke English quite well. I realised that they had to learn a few languages for business purposes.

We booked a room with an attached bath, so we literally got three rooms—a bathroom, a bedroom and a drawing room—all very well arranged. The rate was 50 liras (about ten rupees) per head, per day. After a wash and some tea with bread and jam, we ordered rice and curry for dinner. I thought that they would mess up everything but the food tasted like home fare. There was bright light outside when we had our dinner. Women kept on staring at me, probably because of my sari. After dinner we went to bed.

25th June. When we informed the manager of the hotel that we wanted to look around in the city, he immediately called Thomas Cook and soon a covered car with a guide arrived. We first visited the Milan Cathedral which, though four hundred years old, is incomplete and still being constructed. It looked beautiful with lovely paintings on the window panes. Inside, there were replicas of many Popes. The lace filigree work of their robes was so intricately carved out of white marble that it gave the illusion of real cloth. The stone pillars were beautifully carved and everything was highly polished. After that, we went to see another church that was also very old and though made of bricks, wood, sand and lime mortar, it was rather attractive. There were several water-colour paintings on the walls, the colours still very bright. Among them was the famous painter Leonardo da Vinci's 'The Last Supper'.

On the way I asked the guide how many languages he knew. He replied, 'Seven. Since we deal with tourists from different countries, we need to be jovial at all times and know several languages.' After that we visited the Milan Arcade. The entire market was covered with coloured glass, which let in sufficient light but blocked the heat of the sun. The guide told us that the silk available here was a favourite item for the fashionable elite. In Italy, the metre is used instead of the yard and forty inches make one metre. I purchased a few metres of silk. A man came near our car selling different kinds of brooches. In the meantime a lot of people just surrounded me on the street, observing me and mentioning the word 'Indiano'. Though I could not understand their language, it was clear from their gestures that they were scrutinising me from head to foot. At last, after receiving a shout from the guide they made way for me to enter the car. From the books that they were carrying in their hands, I assumed that they probably moved towards their school. The more we toured Italy, the more we became aware of the rusticity of most of the people here. I will narrate some incidents later.

Our next visit was to the graveyard where all the rich

and eminent people of the country were buried. The garden was full of flowers and marble statues. A photograph of the person was taken at the time of his death, then an identical statue was carved in stone and placed above the grave. It seemed as if the people were too reluctant to leave their worldly pleasures so they were represented as they had lived with an open Bible in their hands. Everyone seemed to be in a situation as described in *Chikitsa Sankat*, where the inanimate would would come alive after being served the miraculous tablet that brought the dead alive—*janto bori*—of the ayurvedic doctor called Tarini Kabiraj.[1] This was a memorable sight. We were told that the poor and ordinary people had a different kind of a graveyard but we could not visit them due to paucity of time. We came back to the hotel, picked up our bags, and headed for the station to board the train for Lugano.

[1] *Chikitsa Sankat* is the well known satirical story written in the 1920s by Durgabati's uncle, Raj Sekhar Basu, a chemist by profession, who wrote under the pseudonym of Parashuram. In the story we have a character called Nando who goes to various doctors for treatment of his ailments but the doctors cannot diagnose the cause of his ailments. Among them is an Indian traditional doctor called Tarini Kabiraj who was said to produce such miraculous tablets that could bring the dead to life.

Three

The train, resembling the Assam Mail in our country, had a corridor. The seats were quite comfortable, covered with soft velvet. This was a second-class coach; there was also a first class one where only the high and mighty travelled. Ordinary people like us usually travelled in the second class. There was also a sleeping car facility for the rich where beds, furnishings, towels etc. were all provided. Here we had to relax all night on the chair with the help of cushions. These cushions were rented out at each station for a couple of liras. You could pick one up and throw it away once you reached the station—the company would have it collected, change the cover and loan it again. I have seen this arrangement across the continent. An acquaintance of ours had lived abroad for quite a few years. He thought that this was a common practice even in India and so once, while travelling from Benaras to Calcutta, he had kept shouting for such pillows.

We are now leaving the Italian border and entering Switzerland. The scenery on both sides is very beautiful and I stood outside the coach holding the corridor railing watching the lake by which the train was moving. There were steamers on the lake and motorcars on the other side. Many other people also stood on the corridor. Occasionally they kept on staring at me and conversing in their own language. From the words 'Gandhi-Tagore' and 'Indiano' I presumed they were concerned about my Indianness. We were all looking outside at the profusion of flowers of various colours everywhere. Sometimes we bought ripe cherries that were being sold at stations. The ice cream vendor was shouting, 'gelati, gelati'. Having spent a few days in Italy I had picked up some Italian words—asking the price of something as—'Con tre lira?' or 'duo' for two. This word was similar to 'dui' in Bangla.

We had crossed the Italian territory so in one station the customs people came to check our luggage. After inspection, they asked for 'tabac'—i.e., whether we were carrying tobacco products. Finding nothing of the sort, they were very curious about the half-used bottle of *Jabakusum*[1] oil, wondering what kind of spirit it was. We gestured that it was hair oil but they were not satisfied. Then they became curious about the big gallon jar of drinking water. We had to open the tap and show them and then they were relieved.

Whenever we crossed a border, the customs officers came to inspect the luggage to see whether there was any kind of spirit or essence like hair lotion, Eau-de-cologne, perfume; any kind of tobacco product like cigar or cigarette; too much of silk material; camera, binoculars etc. A lot of explanation was required for them. Of course, they were a bit lenient if the things were partly used. One person was not allowed to carry more than fifty cigarettes. An acquaintance of ours who was a heavy smoker had made a plan. He kept fifty cigarettes in his own box and another fifty in his wife's box. When the customs officer questioned him he replied that both husband and wife smoked equally. Seeing no tobacco with us they thought that we were heavy drinkers and that is why the water jar made them so suspicious. Upon realising that it contained 'plain' water they considered us immature because people here hardly drank water. They usually drank cheap beer.

[1] *Jabakusum*, a very popular brand of hair oil produced in Calcutta was used by both men and women in most middle-class households at the time. Red in colour and with a distinctive smell, it ensured thick and luscious growth and its popularity had made it into an almost generic term.

We had boarded the train at Milan after lunch. It was late afternoon when we reached Lugano. The train halted for a short time there. Since porters were not easily available, we carried our own luggage—while one person pushed the big boxes through the open windows of the corridor, the other pulled it down. Someone from the hotel was waiting for us at the station and we walked along with him to the hotel that was next to the lake. The old manager told us quite diplomatically that we were given a lake-facing room at a very cheap price. Later I discovered that there was nothing special about it. One could watch the natural beauty surrounding the lake from the balcony of each room. May be such words were part of their trade. We stayed here for one night. The rooms were well-arranged and we had our dinner on the terrace when there was broad daylight outside. After dinner we wandered around places nearby, bought a few small souvenirs from a stationery shop. As we walked around, we could see women looking at us from their windows and calling us 'Indianos'. This hotel in Lugano was called Hotel Weizacruz. The maid here broke the tap of our water gallon jar and when we complained to the manager, she completely denied it. Hence, we had to pay separately for the repairs undertaken.

After breakfast we asked the manager to make arrangements for our sightseeing. He suggested that we travel for some time around the lake in a car and then go to Salvatore by the funicular rail. A motor car arrived and since we did not speak Italian or French, the hall porter instructed the chauffeur accordingly. After moving around the lake we came to the station where many other people were also waiting for the train to Salvatore. A car that looked like a cross between a tram and a bus came sliding down from above the hill and we boarded it. There were twenty-four passengers in all and two people had to share each seat.

The car, run by electricity, started ascending the mountain at a slanted angle. After some time it reached a small flat area where a similar train was waiting to take us further up.

We boarded the second car and the passengers who were waiting to go down climbed the first one. They started descending, and like a lizard climbing a wall we moved upwards. The seats in the earlier coach faced each other but here the seats resembled shelves fixed upon the wall. As we moved upwards, the scenery below appeared smaller and smaller and the snow-capped mountains at a distance became clearer. This was the funicular rail. It soon reached the top and we got down. We were told that the return journey would commence in an hour. Iron fences were planted on the edge of the mountain-top. We were wonderstruck on seeing the scenery all around us! The mountain peaks at the distance reflected the sun's rays and glittered. Far below, the houses and the church steeples of Lugano resembled houses made of cards. Cars, looking like toys, were moving around the shores of the blue lake; the trains looked like toy trains too. The vegetable fields seemed like green carpets spread out. Salvatore was situated six thousand feet above sea level. We acquainted ourselves with an old gentleman, who was not an Englishman but could speak English well. He asked us, 'Did you study in England from childhood? How can you speak such good English?' We told him that in India, English had to be learnt for various reasons. But I do not know English that well and manage to speak it like broken Hindi. The man told me that he had read the English translations of Tagore's *Gitanjali* and I felt happy. About an hour later, we returned to our hotel, paid all the bills and left for the station to go to Lucerne.

We are on our way to Lucerne. Our train is frequently passing through tunnels, some of which are five to seven miles long. The lights in the compartment are on, the windowpanes tightly shut. We just crossed the St. Gotthard tunnel which was nine miles long. The scenery around is beautiful—mountains on both sides with shining snow peaks. Waterfalls and rivers, flowers and fruit trees like cherries and grapes—I am dazed. In the many stations we stopped at on our way, we ate a lot of cherries. They were delicious! At last, we reached Lucerne. We had left our house in Calcutta on the 11th of June, and today was the 26th. We visited so many different places in the last fifteen days. The street in front was very neat and clean. A Swiss milkman walked below the verandah of our room along with a few healthy-looking cows and calves. We washed and changed our clothes and came down to meet an acquaintance from the ship who was speaking to the manager in his office. He was staying at some other hotel but seeing a familiar face after so many days made us happy. This hotel was a bit more decorative and slightly more expensive too. Thomas Cook had given us its address. All the hotels here did not have provision for rooms with attached bath and the ones that did have so were naturally more expensive. The ones without it had just a washbasin with hot and cold water supply in their bedroom. They also provided four small towels. All the rooms were fitted with hot water pipes to keep them warm in winter. None of the hotels in the continent provided soap and one had to pay extra for it.

There was only one person having lunch in the dining room and the manager told us that apart from the two of us, he was the only other man staying in the hotel right now. We summoned the head chef and asked him whether he could make mutton curry for us. At first he kept on staring at our faces and when I told him that it had to be made with curry powder, he gave a smile and said, 'Oh curry, curry—that I know very well.' We were told that some Indian lady had come and stayed at this hotel in Lucerne and she had taught the chef to prepare chicken, mutton and rabbit curry along with *pulao*. He brought and showed me a bottle of curry powder too. I felt assured that he would be able to serve us rice and curry the next day.

The Rigi and Piletus in Lucerne

On the morning of 27th June we went for a walk and then hired a taxi to show us around. The city of Lucerne was situated on the hilltop hence cars, trams, buses etc. were all plying there and both the cars and the drivers looked quite sturdy. We even travelled for an hour in a steamer on the lake. There were hotels on all sides of the lake with evening tea-joints and dance bars, swimming pools, clubs and flower gardens. An hour later we came to a place called Vijlau from where a funicular train took us to the top of Mount Rigi at the height of 5905 feet. While going there, my ears were getting blocked. On reaching the top we found a big flat area with a huge hotel. Plenty of souvenir shops were selling small wooden things—beads, wooden boxes painted with Swiss scenery, trays, pictures, etc. I bought two small wooden toys. Outside the hotel big umbrellas were fixed on the compound under which tables and chairs were laid out. We sat under one such umbrella and had tea and cakes. We enjoyed the surrounding scenery and were told that if the sky was clearer one could see the famous Black Forest of Germany from here. We went back to the hotel by the same route.

Train track amidst the Rigi Mountains

During dinner the Swiss chef brought our long-desired curry and rice. I was dumbstruck at the sight of the tray. On it was a large plate of steaming half-boiled meat and rice and on another plate was some curry powder mixed with water. This was his idea of preparing good curry—he thought we would pour the liquid over the meat and have it. Though I was annoyed at first, later on I realised that I myself was to be blamed for such greed of wanting to have Indian food abroad.

The next day, on 28th of June we went sightseeing in a tourist bus along with a guide from Thomas Cook & Company. At first we visited a hundred-year old building that was still decorated as it was in its earlier years with old furniture and vessels. It gave us an idea of how the Swiss people lived then. There are such old houses in our country too but for generations, no one has cared to maintain them and so nobody visits them. We were then taken to another place that was somewhat dark inside and on a rounded wall was painted a beautiful picture of a war. The picture was 12,400 square feet in size with electric lamps focused on it in such a manner that one would mistake the people in the picture for living beings. It depicted the war between France and Prussia from 1870 to 1871 and showed the French General Bourbaki entering Switzerland with his huge army. On one side we saw the Swiss and the French army fighting against the Prussians. There were several ambulances all round. Dead and mutilated soldiers and horses lay scattered here and there. Interestingly, a few real ambulances and original clothes used by the soldiers in the actual war were also displayed in such a manner that they also seemed to be part of the picture. Had not the guide pointed it out, we would perhaps not be able to differentiate between the picture and the real artifacts. There were five or six different kinds of people in our group. Among them I could identify the French, the Italian, the German and the English. The guide kept on narrating in different languages.

From here we went to another place on the street to see the statue of a dead lion carved out in white marble in 1821 by a Swiss sculptor named Lucas Ahoin. On the 10th of August, 1712, the people of Paris had attacked the Tuileries Palace of King Louis XVI. The Swiss guards of the palace did not know that the king had already escaped along with his family through a secret passage and they kept on fighting till they were killed. This marble statue of the lion was made in memory of their brave sacrifice. There were several other things that I saw in Lucerne but I cannot recollect. We stayed there for two nights and on the third day started towards Interlaken.

We did not have to pay any rent for our luggage from Genoa to Lucerne but since the train route to Interlaken covered a mountainous terrain, there were weight restrictions and we had to pay for extra luggage. All the trains in Switzerland ran on electricity. Without any engine they just climb up straight on the mountain with a rattling sound. One cannot stand straight inside the train during this period and I felt a certain jolt in my chest and waist when I tried to do so. The scenery around was so beautiful that I did not know what to see and what to leave out. The mountains were covered with green trees, the snow peaks were dazzling white, the colour of the lake deep blue! The snow had just begun to melt and it lay scattered around the mountains as if white laundry had been spread out to dry. Some melted snow had turned into waterfalls. The hectic travel for the last few days had tired us a lot and I was occasionally dozing off. But just so that I do not miss such beautiful scenes, I kept on staring with tired eyes. We reached Interlaken in the evening and the hotel where we put up was called Hotel du Lac. It was quite cold here. It was like winter in our country. We were too tired and thus we did not go anywhere but just changed, dined and slept.

On the morning of 29th June, we made a list of the places we wanted to visit. After breakfast we left for Lotter Brunnen on an electric train along with packed lunch. We saw several waterfalls on both sides of the road. An elderly lady was travelling in the same compartment along with a nineteen-year old boy. He came forward and asked us, ‘Are you from India?’ We said ‘yes’ and also asked him how he recognised us. He said that they were tourists from America and had visited our country and enjoyed it. He introduced us to his mother who enquired whether it was our first trip to

Switzerland. I told her that my husband had been here before but I had come for the first time. The boy added, 'That's why you are liking it so much. But is this place as beautiful as Kashmir? We had been to Kashmir and liked it more than this.' Now I felt uneasy. I had not seen Kashmir whereas a foreigner had seen it. Then I consoled myself that it was not possible to visit every place. I'd surely see Kashmir some time or another.

The train stopped at Lotter Brunnen. We bid farewell to the mother and son, boarded a car for some distance and then walked to Trümmelbach Falls. This waterfall was very beautiful; five different kinds of scenery could be seen in five different stages. Each step had elaborate arrangements for viewing—an electric train, a verandah, an over-bridge, etc. After watching our fill we took a motor car to a place called Sydek and arrived for lunch at 'Sydek Hotel'. Chunks of ice lay scattered around the tables below the verandah and I picked up a chunk to see that it resembled the frozen larder in a sweetmeat shop. There was a mountain in front of us, the frozen peak of which was called Sydek. A train connection from here would take us to the Rhone glacier. Like a bus conductor, the guard of the train also started shouting for passengers, 'Rhone Glacier, Rhone Glacier!' and departed. From the hotel itself I could see the train gradually move upwards in the snow and ultimately disappear into a tunnel. We had not seen this glacier. After lunch we hired a phaeton car—the black horse was quite tall and stout and moved with great speed. The coachman was French but he understood both French and English. We made a contract with him that he would take us to Grindelwald glacier and bring us back to Hotel Sydek within an hour and a half just in time to catch the train for Interlaken.

On reaching the glacier we walked around and saw beautiful flowers of different colours bloom like a multi-

The Trümmelbach Falls

Inside the cave of the Grindelwald Glacier

coloured carpet spread out in front of us. The coachman acted as our guide. The snow of the glacier had levelled the valley between the two mountains and they now seemed like mountains made of chalk. People had carved out a cave in this ice. For four shillings we hired a local Alpine guide who understood English. A small tin shed nearby had skating accessories, spiked shoes, sticks and blankets. We covered ourselves in blankets and took a walking stick in hand while the guide accompanied us with a pickaxe. The cave inside was made of solid ice. Icicles like tree roots were hanging from the roof and the sunrays reflecting on the ice gave the inside a bluish tint. I broke a couple of icicles to see that they were like glass tubes. Some narrow wooden planks were laid on the floor to prevent skidding and the drains on both edges led the gush of water and small pieces of ice outside. I was at first surprised to see trees and flowers inside the cave but later realised that they had been brought from outside for decoration and the ice kept them fresh. I could not reach the end of the cave as the cold had already numbed my nose. Our guide told us that every two or three days the cave had to be axed and kept in shape otherwise the ice blocked up the path. During winter they only skate over the snow and this is known as winter sports. We went back to our phaeton and the coachman drove it quite fast.

On the morning of 30th June we started packing as we had to leave for Paris by an afternoon train. We finished around eleven o' clock and the train was at noon. I had heard about a beautiful garden here which had a strange kind of clock made out of fruit and flower trees. The Swiss are famous for their clocks and we had seen different kinds of clocks in the shops but I was very keen to see this flower clock. My husband at first refused to go but after a lot of coaxing and cajoling he accompanied me. We asked for the directions in English and walked briskly to the garden nearby to find the famous clock. Situated on a little raised ground, the digits of the clock were made of different kinds of flowers and shrubs. The pendulum and the hands of the clock were made of some metal and at the centre there were small wooden figures of two old men with long white beards. It was 11.30 a.m. and as luck favoured us, I saw the smaller figure beat a small drum with the hammer in his hand. The bigger old man did nothing and I presumed that he would do his job on the hour. There were many other things to see in the garden but due to lack of time we returned to the hotel and immediately left for the railway station to board the train for Paris.

8 Four

1st July. Boarding the train at noon on the 30th of June we reached Paris at 10 o'clock at night. It was drizzling when we arrived and there were huge houses and shops on both sides of the street. Since the beauty of Switzerland was still fresh in our minds, we could not appreciate this weather in Paris. It was only after staying here for five days that we could enjoy its appeal. There were no porters at the station. After a lot of effort we found two porters who smelt strongly of alcohol. We requested them to take us to a taxi, which was known as 'automobile' here, and this automobile took us to Hotel St. Petersburg at Rue-de-Camartine. We had booked our accommodation here from Switzerland itself at the rate of ninety francs per day and were given a large room. In Paris we saw the Louvre Museum, the Rodin Museum, the Eiffel Tower, the Luxembourg Gardens, Bois de Boulogne Gardens, etc. One day we even went to Versailles. We also visited the zoo which was very dirty and the animals looked unhealthy. We climbed the thousand feet high Eiffel Tower in a lift. On the top there was a photographer who was ready to take pictures in whichever pose we wanted. There were a few souvenir shops too, selling brass replicas of the tower, picture postcards, etc. Tea was also available.

One day we went to Gallerie Lafayette that was much smaller than the New Market in Calcutta but its arrangements were different. Our feet ached roaming around the picture galleries of the Louvre. Inside the museum, we saw many artists sitting and trying to make copies of the paintings of the great masters. Seeing us, an artist came and offered to make oil portraits for us. For this we needed to stay in Paris for a month and appear for sittings every day. We thanked her for the offer and told her that we were here only for a few days. An interesting thing that we noticed in Paris was that people here sat on chairs and tables on the pavements from morning till midnight and had food and drinks. We had seen such sights occasionally in other parts of the continent too, but not to such an extent as in Paris. One day we went to an opera where acting was entirely through songs. We did not understand French but could follow the storyline from a small booklet that was being sold, that had it translated in English.

The Palace and the gardens of Versailles were very beautiful and we took photographs with a group of tourists here. If one began to describe the intricate tapestry and furniture that adorned the inside of the palace, it would know no end! One evening, after dinner we hired a car for four hours to see the nightlife of Paris. The guide showed us several places. He took us to a small shop-like place. As soon as he knocked on the door an elderly lady opened it and we went inside. To our astonishment, we saw at least a hundred men and women dancing there. There was laughter and a strong smell of alcohol everywhere. I even saw six young Bengali men among the people dancing. I felt sad that their parents who had sent them abroad for higher studies had no idea that they were learning something quite different. Of course dancing has become very popular in our country as well. After staying here for about ten minutes we went elsewhere. A long time ago this place was used as a prison but now it had become a site for entertainment for all the good-for-nothing people. There were songs, dances, theatre and tableaus going on inside. Further down the road we came to a huge building that from its external appearance seemed to have offices and shops on each floor but had a totally different ambience in the basement. Here too, the front door was closed. After we rang the bell a servant opened it and about twenty-five of us entered the lobby. Going down two floors we seemed to enter a big city where people were busy shopping, dancing, singing, swimming, etc. An artificial lake, along with houses similar to those of Venice, had been created and couples dressed in Italian clothes were singing love songs. Some scantily dressed dancers behaved in such a manner as if they had discarded all shame from the moment they were born! The elderly people probably had no right to participate in such merriment, because we saw them seated as observers just like us. The women who were dancing were just like toys in the hands of the expert men. While dancing, they placed them on their shoulders and over their heads as if their bodies did not have any bones and were made of feathers!

When we were very young, we had heard an old domestic in our house say, that a first wife had food left on her husband's plate; the second wife had food sitting with him and the third one would have food sitting on the husband's shoulders. Looking at these dancers I felt that whatever their status as a wife was, why only while eating, their supple bodies made them capable of touring the whole world sitting on men's shoulders. We returned to our hotel at around six in the evening. The entire city of Paris shone bright at night with lights from glow signs and advertisements. Even the Eiffel Tower was decorated with lights. We had seen Paris twice and though I might have missed many things, I am narrating both the visits together. On reading about Paris in books and on hearing about it from different people, I had the idea that Parisians were very aesthetic and refined, neat and clean, but after staying here for a few days I realised that they loved to show off. In the train I saw a well-dressed young woman wearing an expensive lace gown made of silk but her inner garments had not been washed for ages. She stank when we sat next to her. However, before reaching her destination, she meticulously put on red lipstick, applied mascara on her eyes, and taking perfume on her finger tips massaged it on her hands and cheeks. There was no slip there! Even the men stank, but they did not have such cosmetics with them. Not that everyone was like them—but at least eighty per cent of them were. Anyhow, after staying here for five days, we boarded a train for Calais. Crossing the English Channel on a ship that took about an hour, we landed at the English port of Dover. The colour of the water in the English Channel was like moss.

On landing at Dover we had to pass through customs where our luggage was inspected. They enquired where and when we had bought the binoculars. I replied that it belonged to my father-in-law and it was with my husband even in 1923 when he was a student in England. A similar question was posed for the camera. My husband replied that he had bought it at Selfridges in 1924 before returning to India. They were satisfied with both the answers. The next question was whether we had any perfumes or lotions with us and on inspecting the eau-de-cologne, they let us go. There were about two or three customs officers who had laid our luggage in a neat row over their tables. I found an English lady being harassed because she had not declared all the goods she had brought from Paris which included a big bottle of lotion. I do not know what happened to her in the end.

There was a Bengali gentleman who had been in the same railway compartment while coming from Paris. He was looking for us and on locating us said, 'Hurry up! Climb in soon. The train will leave right now.' We jumped in with our luggage. It was a Pullman train. We had our afternoon tea on board and saw the English countryside on both sides. Sometimes in between the fields full of crops were signboards for 'Beecham's Pill' which was like the '*Jarmolin: Jorer Jom*' [Jarmolin: Fever's

Enemy][1] advertisement in our country. Another advertisement made me laugh. There was the head of a healthy-looking cow and below it was written, 'Home-killed. Come and buy a few pieces'. I had heard of the phrase 'home-made' but, 'home-killed' was new to me. After some time the train crossed a bridge over the Thames for a few seconds. So this was the River Thames! Compared to the rivers in our country, it was just like a canal. I was reminded of an incident when an old Indian gentleman, an acquaintance of ours, had come to visit London. Seeing the river from the top of the double-decker bus he had called out loudly for his son-in-law and asked, 'Sudhangshu! Is this your Thames River?'

The train reached Victoria Station in London. It was drizzling constantly and with fog covering the whole area, the houses seemed gloomy and dark in colour. London was like this, I consoled myself. Our friend Arthur Hunter who came to receive us at the station informed us that he had reserved rooms for us at the Royal Palace Hotel next to Kensington Park. We were also told that the London Customs Office had confiscated the two big suitcases that we had directly sent from Genoa because they contained two rolls of silk material. We would have to offer explanation and then free our luggage. The rest of the things were already in our hotel room which was very good. We retired for the day. It was ten o' clock at night and still the rays of the sun seeped through the windows on to our bed. It would be dark only around eleven.

We went to the customs house outside London a couple of days later to fight it out and bring our boxes back. There

[1] Before antibiotics came into vogue, the people of Calcutta had to depend on several medicines to counter the frequent attacks of malaria, typhoid, kaalazar and other diseases. Big hoardings in streets would advertise them. Like quinine, Jarmolin was also a very well-known brand of medicine promising to cure fever.

were two sari borders which they called rolls of silk. Another Godavari cotton sari seemed to them to be made of artificial silk. This was the extent to which their knowledge of silk went! Again, there was a box of tooth powder that they suspected to be cocaine. When we angrily replied that they could send it to some laboratory for investigation, they let us go. The last two days had been quite cold but it grew warmer as soon as the sun shone brightly. The weather here was very unpredictable. Sometimes it felt hot, at other times, when it rained it was very damp.

A few days later we went to meet my father's friend, the famous psychologist Dr Ernest Jones. He enquired a lot about our country and asked us to write to my father on his behalf inviting him to London. He also invited us for lunch one day. While discussing several things Dr Jones asked us, 'We have so many Indian things in the British Museum here in London. If you ever win *Swaraj*, will you take them back?'

'I don't know what we will do then,' I replied.

Dr Jones told us that whenever Dr Colonel Berkeley Hill from the Ranchi Mental Hospital visited London, he would be his guest. Dr Jones took good care of us and we too got to know many things from him.

One day we went to visit Lincoln's Inn and the Law Court. Since women in our country did not get much opportunity to see what happens inside our High Court, I did not wish to lose the opportunity here. One day we also visited the Privy Council. At that time a session was going on concerning property matters of some Indian gentleman. While listening to the counsel, the judge suddenly interjected, 'You are saying that Brajakishore died when he was about eighteen or nineteen. How can you talk about his son? Can a person have a son at eighteen?'

The advocate counsel replied, 'I've heard that in Bengal,

boys would be married off at fourteen or fifteen. So, being a father at eighteen is not an impossibility.'

At this, there was a roar of laughter in the courtroom. I saw the Late Sir Dinshaw Mullah also in the judge's seat during this time.

The British police were something to look at. They had to be six feet tall. One could always ask street directions from them. The streets of London were full of people and cars. I have seen innumerable cars, trams, buses, the public always abiding, and the police controlling everything efficiently. Because of the huge amount of cars on the roads, there were subways for pedestrians to cross the street at ease. The stairs used to climb down were fitted with electric lights. Inside the subways there were bookstalls, fruit stalls, Swan & Edgar stores and also branches of several big shops. Once inside, it was difficult to imagine what was happening outside. If one needed to use the toilet, one could put in a penny in the slot of a closed door and it would open automatically. An old lady sitting in front of that toilet would collect the pennies meant to keep it clean. Though she sat knitting, she also kept a sharp eye on people trying to open the door without dropping a penny. An acquaintance of ours had once somehow managed to get in without paying any money but was caught red-handed by the old woman when he came out.

The buses here are very comfortable. They have soft cushioned seats and all of them are double-deckers. People who smoke in the bus are supposed to sit upstairs, causing less inconvenience to other passengers. Our jovial friend Sir Abaninath Mitra and his wife arrived from Berlin a few days after us and we were very happy to visit the museums with them. The street was called Exhibition Road and the houses on both sides had various exhibitions and museums. We saw the War Museum, Victoria & Albert Museum, the Natural History Museum amongst others, all of which were worth seeing!

One day we went travelling by bus somewhere. An English lady was sitting next to me along with her young son. The boy was playing and had somehow dirtied himself. The educated mother instantly took out her handkerchief, spat on a corner and wiped her son's face clean. Another day, I saw some labourers digging the roads with pickaxes. On hearing a sound I found them spitting on the palms of their hands and rubbing them together as one does while washing with soap. They then took out their handkerchiefs from their pockets and wiped their hands. I have also seen people using their spit to stick stamps on envelopes, to remove stains from their overcoats, to seal envelopes, etc. These are the same people who take pride in calling themselves educated and civilised! Even the scavengers and sweepers in our country who are constantly cleaning dirt would never like to clean their children's faces or their own hands with spit. One day I saw a dirty beggar boy on the street, his face blackened with grime. Poor boy! I thought, his face perhaps would be covered with spit today!

Though the streets were quite crowded, people did not unnecessarily push each other or bicker among themselves. There were no fruit peels or torn pieces of paper lying on the streets. Netted bins were fixed on trees for waste disposal. Even in front of the cinema or theatre halls people waited patiently in queues like silent mechanical dolls, without any irritation or displeasure. These are things we should learn.

People who returned to India after staying in England often commented that the English women were much more hard-working than our women at home. I had cherished a desire to learn such English habits but once I was here I realised that English women, if they were to work like us, they would never have been able to compete with us. I will give you the reasons. First of all, people could work more here because it was a cold country. Secondly, in India people usually lived in a joint family. There was a difference in working according to personal convenience as against that for the benefit of others or only after seeking permission to do so from the elders in the family. Moreover, back in India, there was no question of having meals on time. The men in the house might have some fixed time for meals during the weekdays but on holidays they might delay so much that it would be evening by the time the kitchen would be cleaned. Here such things are not possible as one had to eat according to the convenience of the person cooking and serving the food. No one would allow one person to have lunch at ten o'clock and another at one o'clock. Also one did not need a helping hand to chop different vegetables or grind various kinds of spices. Some soup, fried fish, meat or boiled vegetables and a little pudding was enough for lunch. The problem of washing hands every time one cooked vegetarian and non-vegetarian items did not exist here. Whatever was cooked was shared equally among married women, widows, single women and children. If someone was a vegetarian, he or she did not need to be served on separate utensils after washing one's hands. All these reasons made things less time consuming here. Of course one must not think that just because I am criticising our Indian habits, they are all bad. I am just mentioning them for a comparative analysis. In England, after the husband leaves for work, the wife becomes busy doing several other things apart from housework. She might be speaking to different prospective tenants for her ground floor apartment and sending out flowers from her garden for sale. The different people she encounters in this process are not screened by her husband who goes out with the wife after returning from work at the end of the day. Both men and women here understand the need for taking care of their health and so work as well as enjoy themselves accordingly. How many people in our country have such a comprehensive understanding?

I have seen how meat and vegetables are sold in shops here. Ox ribs, liver, intestines, tongue etc. are separately packed up in cabbage leaves and displayed in the glass counters. One pineapple costs three shillings here, a peach in one shilling and banana six pence per piece. You can even buy finger chips sold in thin paper envelopes.

People in this country have less attachment towards material objects. And why not? No one possesses things personally. A hotel building might belong to somebody; the furniture to someone else; the bedding and linen to another person. I don't know whether it is true but I've heard that even clothes were available on hire. Parents looked after their children till they were capable of working. They then moved out and got married. If sons or daughters kept on staying at their parents' home, most parents would want money as rent or food expenses.

One day we went by train from London to Acton to visit a biscuit factory. On that day 'Nice' biscuits were being made. Necessary quantities of flour, sugar, eggs, butter and grated coconut were being mixed in a big wooden vat. Then with the help of some electrical gadgets they were rolled out into cushion-like shapes. A large knife cut each of them into four pieces and then each was put beneath another machine that rolled it out in a thin layer. This thin sheet was continuously moving under another machine with saws from where they emerged in the shape of the biscuit. These then went into a huge cupboard like chamber where they were baked and eventually came out in trays. During the whole process, one person stood in front of the machines and continuously sprinkled sugar on the dough. The woman whom I saw sprinkling sugar had well-built arms, probably as a result of the continuous exercise. All the fat women in our country who are keen to have a shapely figure can try out such arm exercises. The women worked here from 8 a.m. to 5 p.m. with a couple of hours' break in between. The factory manager gifted us some freshly baked biscuits that tasted completely different from the ordinary ones.

In London there is a restaurant on Gerrard Street (it is Gerrave Street in Bengali) owned by a Muslim man called Sophis and named after him. His European widow now runs this place and all the waiters here are Indian Muslims. All kinds of Indian dishes like fish *kaliya*,[2] curry, meat kofta kebabs, shammi kebab, biriyani, pulao, chops,[3] chapatti, parathas, jalebis, cheese cakes etc. were prepared here. All these items were served hot and they were very polite in their behaviour. One day we tasted their shrimp and brinjal curry and it tasted quite good. We could only consume a quarter of the amount that we thought we could eat—two chapattis were enough. But the people who come to work in this country have become so used to having curry and rice that the taste of the food here does not appeal to them anymore. Whenever I went to eat at this hotel, I found that the foreigners were more eager to have food here than the Indians. They consumed four times more food than us and the price of four shillings per head (i.e., about two rupees twelve annas) was quite steep.

One day we visited Croydon, Eastbourne and Brighton. People could fly from Croydon to Karachi. Eastbourne and Brighton were places by the sea, but the sea here did not have waves—it was rather still and unappealing. A lot of people came here to sunbathe.

One day we went to visit Cambridge. About ten or twelve colleges comprised of the Cambridge University—Kings's

[2] Fish is the most favourite Bengali dish and is prepared in different forms and tastes. Among them is the *kaliya* which is a spicy preparation done with big slices of sweet water fish cooked in a thick gravy made of onions and other spices.

[3] The 'chop' resembling the croquet is used as a common snack.

College, Emmanuel College, Downing College, etc. There was a strict instruction that students had to seek permission from their hostel wardens if they ventured out into the streets after ten o'clock at night. The students were always occupied and excited by activities like swimming, football, running and jumping. King Henry VIII of England had founded the King's College and portraits of the English poets who studied here like Byron, Tennyson and others hung on the wall. It nearly always drizzles in London and there is hardly any sunshine. So the day the sun shines it becomes rather auspicious here. Small children go out to play in the open fields to play wearing sleeveless clothes. The elders leave their regular work and sunbathe wherever the sun shines; the middle-aged lovers go punting and the young just enjoy themselves in whichever manner possible. A little strong sunshine after a few days made us feel hot. There were 'Happy Boy' and endless other ice cream carts on the streets. People got impatient with the heat, newspapers were full of articles related to the 'heat wave'. Swimming costumes were sold aplenty. Men and women spent their days in the lake at Regent Park. One day, unable to bear the heat, a young girl went inside the fountain in Trafalgar Square and we heard that the police had arrested her.

One day we went for a stroll at the Kew Gardens here which resembled our Botanical Gardens with its variety of flowers and even its pagoda. There is a zoo called Whipsnade Zoological Garden that is thirty miles away from London. Animals are kept here in the open and it took us an entire day to see the whole of it. It was worth a watch. During winter months the animals here are sent to the Regent Park Zoo in London, which was also not bad. Here the lions and tigers are fed with salt and cabbage leaves along with their raw meat. May be like the Englishmen, the tigers here are also used to having salad with their meals. This zoo is smaller in size to our Alipore Zoo, but the aquarium inside was worth seeing. Fish, crabs and turtles from the rivers and the seas were kept in environs that resembled their natural habitat. Fresh salt water was continuously supplied to the sea fish section while the river fish had only clear water. Corals were also preserved in a very fine way. One had to buy separate tickets to enter the aquarium. It was dark inside with lights arranged only at the spots meant to be highlighted and we were surprised to see such a wide variety of design and colour of the fish. Smoking was not allowed inside.

One day we took a train to Coventry. From there a motor coach took us to Kenilworth Castle—the one made famous by Sir Walter Scott's novel *Kenilworth.* It resembled our Lucknow Residency building. We then visited Stratford-Upon-Avon—the birthplace of Shakespeare. The bard's letters written in his own hand and many other things that he used were displayed in this museum. There is also a theatre at Stratford called Shakespeare Memorial Theatre. A few

Shakespeare's birthplace: Stratford-upon-Avon

years ago this theatre was burned down and it has been reconstructed. The bard's plays are staged here.

On our return journey we saw the Warwick Castle at Coventry that was beautiful both from the outside as well as inside. It reminded us of a bygone era. London and its suburbs do not resemble old historical pictures but the Warwick Castle was historical. The story goes that Ethelfleda, daughter of Alfred the Great built this castle on the shore of the Avon River in the city of Warwick to protect it from the plundering of the Danes. 'Victorious William' had fortified the external walls of the fort, but Edward III built new walls and strengthened its towers.

We entered the fort. A group of people waited in the corridor with a call bell in front with the words WAIT FOR GUIDE inscribed on it. After waiting for a while, a guide came and took us around the rooms on both floors. The hall was big but the state bedroom and the drawing room were the best. It was nice to look at the Avon River from the red sitting room. The dining hall, with oil paintings on its walls, was magnificient. Having seen the Warwick Castle, we came back to Coventry and reached London by train at around 9 p.m.

After staying in the hotel for a week we arranged for a cheaper place to stay. Two rooms in a residential house were available but not with separate bath and toilet. I noticed that most houses in London had plenty of rooms but only a single bath and toilet. In our country members of a large family might be forced to use only one toilet and bath but this is permissible because we are much neater than them. We can clean our toilets by pouring a lot of water on the floor but that is not possible here because there is no outlet for water to be drained out. If one wanted to clean the floor one fixed a wet duster at the end of a long brush and scrubbed the floor. There were big tubs for washing and bathing which were fitted with taps on the inside. But one did not like to use the same tub that five others had used earlier. In the hotels too, these common baths are kept as clean as possible and whenever we rented rooms with attached baths we often cleaned them with phenyl. Thus, after a few days in this house we felt uncomfortable and returned to the hotel once again.

We would visit the Thomas Cook office every week to collect our mail from India. There was a provision in that office to sit down and reply to those letters. Tables, chairs, ink, pens, envelopes and paper were all provided and we just had to pay for the postage.

There are many Bengali students in London and we would often meet them on the streets. The suburbs of the city were prettier than the city itself. The small village houses and the flower gardens were very neatly laid out. During our stay here it became quite hot like the months of March and April back home. We heard from people here, that London was experiencing such a hot weather after several years. We therefore did not need to use the woollen clothes that we carried with us.

Moving around in the streets and in public transport I noticed that women travelled much more than men. If there were thirty people in a bus, twenty-five or twenty-six of them would be women. I've heard from people here that after many men lost their lives in the last World War, the ratio of women as compared to men in London was proportionately more. It was the same in the continent too.

Except for the people who have returned from India, people on an average, and especially women, ate much less. They may subsist on a few glasses of beer, an apple and two slices of bread for the whole day. Not that everyone ate that way, but most of them did. A young man belonging to our neighbourhood in Kolkata had come to study in London.

He described the manner in which ordinary women in London lived and I am narrating it almost verbatim. Waking up in the morning, she would hurriedly have a cup of tea, put on a shiny coat on top of the dirty dress she would normally wear, dab rouge on her cheeks and red lipstick on her lips, put on a hat, and leave for work. After working for the whole day, she would come home and just have two buns. Her boyfriend would then arrive. She would dress up again and leave for some place where they would dance for the whole night and come home around four in the morning. Since no cooking was done at home, her boyfriend would treat her at some cheap place for dinner worth two shillings.

I have already mentioned the London subway and now will tell you about the underground railway system. It might be fair to call the entire city of London hollow. People walk under the ground; so do certain types of trains known as the metropolitan railway. Except for one or two coaches, smoking is banned on the entire train. It goes through dark tunnels and there are electric lights in the compartments. Sometimes one can see daylight for a few seconds. Then there are the tube stations which are thousands of feet below the ground—I do not know how many. Earlier they had lifts operating from the street level but now with scientific development, these lifts have been replaced by escalators. You do not have to make any effort to climb up or down. Just stand on the first step and the machine will do the job, taking you where you want to go. Gradually you reach the platform, each step giving way onto another. At that moment, you would only feel a slight jerk in your body. The dark tunnels underneath were spread out throughout the entire city like serpents. They even went underneath the Thames River. This is called the tube and one or two trains came rushing in at five-minute intervals. The doors open and close automatically and people hop in and out quickly. Inside there are notices stating that smoking is 'strictly prohibited'. These tube trains move in three or four tiers under the earth. In each tube station there is a provision of fresh air and one could feel it gushing out at certain specific spots on the platform.

One day two young boys about seven or eight years old were trying to board the train along with us. Somehow one of them got left out on the platform and the door closed. He shouted to the other boy and asked him to wait at the next station. If this happened in our country the boy would probably be in tears. The boys here have such practical sense because their parents leave them on their own from a very early age.

The tube trains are always very crowded because one can reach one's destination very quickly. Often one cannot get a seat and has to stand for the entire stretch of the journey by holding on to the leather handles hanging from the ceiling.

Beggars are not permitted to ask for alms openly, so they play something to entertain people. Sometimes they draw flowers or different scenes on the pavement using coloured chalk and expect the passersby to drop some coins. Sometimes they gather in groups and perform like concert parties with flutes, drums, etc. These beggars are slightly upper class and initially I was often surprised seeing them in hats, coats and ties. There is another system of begging too. I have seen women standing at street corners or underneath trees with some matchboxes spread out on a big tray. When they ask you to buy a match box you pay them whatever you wish and then return the matchbox too. A Bengali boy had once asked a beggar playing a violin why he did not perform at some theatre. The beggar had informed him that he earned three times more by begging than he would have working in a theatre.

There are plenty of advertisements of Indian curry powder on the streets of London. I have seen the picture of an *Odiya* cook with his hair tied in a knot above his head squatting on the floor and grinding spices on the mortar and pestle.

One day we went to see the tunnel beneath the River Thames along with Abani babu and his wife. A tube which was illuminated by electric lights had been fixed underground. Trams, buses, cars and people move through the tunnel constantly. There was no way one could make out that a river flowed above. There was a spiral iron staircase at the end of the tunnel. While climbing up the steps, I remember counting them and it was two hundred and seventy five in number. On reaching the top we were surrounded by a group of young boys who pestered us for pennies. They looked like slum dwellers and followed us on the streets too. They grew in number as we proceeded and sometimes they shouted, 'Oh, look at them John, they are Indians!' Sometimes their parents scolded them and tried to stop them but they were unwilling to listen. A few small girls touched our saris and said, 'Beautiful,' but the boys noticed nothing and just kept on screaming, 'Give us pennies!' Abani babu tried to ward them off by raising his walking stick but they went back to square one again. Sometimes the elders in the group also behaved like the children with the exception that they were slightly more restrained. Windows on both sides of the street opened for people to have a look at us, as if we were street performers ready to perform antics with our trained bears. We were ultimately relieved when we boarded the bus.

One day we went to visit the Hippodrome Theatre in London. On that day the story of 'The Pitcher and the Demon' from the *Arabian Nights* was being enacted. A demon or jinn with a green beard encircled with dark green clouds emerged from a small green pitcher and then floated in the air over the stage and above the heads of the audience. When it came over my head I noticed that it was hanging about thirty feet above but could not make out the mechanism that made it float in the air.

There is another kind of performance called 'Non-stop Variety' that takes place in London. It usually begins at a particular hour and continues till midnight. It combines dance, music, theatre and tableau and one could buy a ticket for the show anytime and stay till it was over. However, if you came out, you would have to buy a ticket again. One day, I had seen a mime performance here where the actors on the stage only made gestures while another person standing on one side narrated the whole story for the audience. On another occasion we watched a 'casanova' performance in the theatre. The whole stage went on revolving and we saw houses, rivers, boats with at least a hundred people performing together.

One day we went to visit Madame Tussaud's Museum where the French lady had created many beautiful wax figures of different people and displayed them in an exhibition. These figures are so natural that they seem to be alive and real. After buying an entrance ticket I asked the policeman on duty near the staircase the direction to the exhibition hall. When he did not reply, I noticed that his eyelids were not moving. Inside the hall there were figures of the Royal family, Mahatma Gandhi, all the great writers of Europe, poets, sportspersons, etc. We had to buy separate tickets for going down to the 'Chamber of Horror' in the basement. After purchasing tickets we observed the faces of the two policemen sitting on both sides of the entrance more meticulously. They were identical and it was difficult to figure out which was real and which a replica. After observing one face for some time the real one smiled and showed us the way.

I was quite depressed by the display below—especially the figures of thieves, scoundrels, murderers and dacoits. There were also models showing how people were punished in those days—some were hanged from the ceiling with a noose round their necks, some were about to be guillotined; the fear and fright writ on their faces was unimaginable. Someone had killed a child in the city of London and the dead body was found in a pram. The skeleton of that small child and his faded clothes were still displayed here along with the pram! Who will not feel depressed seeing such things? There were covered screens in some places on which were inscribed 'For Adults Only'. Unable to restrain my curiosity, I lifted one such screen and saw a man pierced with a sword hanging upside down. Red blood continuously flowing from his wound, it trickled down to his mouth and hair. All these depressing sights recurred in my mind and in front of my eyes throughout that day. What strange taste these Englishmen had! According to Sri Rangin Haldar, all these things displayed were the manifestations of the demonic qualities in men.

We would occasionally go for a stroll to Regent Park. There were plenty of big trees here that were full of pigeons. People here have a great attachment towards birds and beasts, the maximum being for dogs and black cats. They believe that black cats bring good luck and prosperity to people who own them. People come here along with their children and their pets. Once a Bengali boy told me how he had once shooed a cat away from his bedroom. This had angered her old landlady to such a great extent that she had cursed him, 'You will never pass your examination.' She kept both dogs and cats and took the dogs for a stroll in the morning. Meat was brought for them from the market. In the evening the cat would be taken for a stroll in a pram and arrangements for fish were also done.

While strolling in Regent Park one day I saw a man sitting on a bench chewing peanuts. A lot of pigeons were moving around his feet. Sometimes he would eat and at other moments would sit quietly with a grin on his face. What was that for, I wondered. What kind of behaviour was this in a civilised society? Since it was impolite to stand and watch him, I went and sat down on a nearby bench. I then realised that he was holding a peanut between his teeth and a pigeon would come and sit on his shoulder and peck at it with its beak. This was happiness for him! While sitting on the bench I also observed other people. Small children always ran about and therefore felt thirsty. There were drinking water taps in the park from which water continuously came out. A bowl was fixed to the tap with chains and the children would drink from there. This was not good for health. Public lectures would also be held at Regent Park.

One day, I went to see the Westminster Abbey. Though it was quite good to look at, it was not as appealing as the Italian churches. Aristocrats and royals as well as ordinary citizens get married in this church. There were graves of those belonging to royalty too. In fact the inner hall was full of people's graves. They did not have headstones and one could find the names carved out on the cement floor, which people were constantly trampling over. I felt hesitant to do so and tried my level best to bypass them while walking. This was the first time I saw anybody walk over dead people. The Westminster Abbey did not look as good as it appeared in a picture.

Five

We left London for Paris on the 23rd of August. Mr Jitendra Mohan Sen and his wife accompanied us. We travelled together from Paris to Vienna and the four of us spoke in Bengali to our heart's content. We had left London at eleven in the morning and arrived in Paris at ten past six in the evening. Mr Hunter, Abani babu and a few other acquaintances came to see us off at Victoria Station. On reaching France our permits were checked, our luggage examined. This time we stayed in Paris for three days. On the fourth day we left for Brussels, the capital of Belgium, and reached at around 9 a.m. From the station we went to our hotel, had breakfast, and left on a tour by a motor bus. Our guide in this trip was a very jovial person. He kept entertaining us with a lot of jokes along the way.

The streets of Belgium are very neat and clean. Our bus went through the national forest here and the scene was quite beautiful. There were woods on either side of the tar-laid road. Sunlight seeping through the tall trees in the woods on both sides of the road created a strange greenish reflection. Our bus soon reached Waterloo, the battlefield of Napoleon. A sprawling field, where the war was fought lay in front of us. There were three or four buildings around it, which were used as hospitals at the time of the war. Like the huge picture we saw at Lucerne, there was a huge panoramic painting of the Battle of Waterloo here. One guide came forward to explain the meaning of this picture to us. There were people belonging to five different races in our group—there were four Bengalis including us, three or four Englishmen, two Italians, five or six Germans and a few French ladies. The way these young ladies laughed and joked among themselves irritated the guide who was forced to ask them, 'Have you come here to see anything or do you want to create commotion?' This chiding brought the ladies back to their senses and they became quiet. The guide resumed his explanation of the painting without any further interruptions.

In remembrance of the dead soldiers who fought in the war, the women of Waterloo had scraped out a layer of soil from the entire battlefield and created a pyramid out of it. There were 314 steps to climb to the top of this mausoleum that had a replica of Napoleon on its summit. The War Museum in Brussels is worth visiting. It contains all the weapons and clothes used by the Europeans in the past World War. Things like how the soldiers lived in the trenches and how poisonous gas was used were explained clearly. During the war, a German nurse named Edith Kevel was sentenced to death because she had been found guilty of serving an English soldier. The guide pointed to an open field and said, 'This is where Edith Kevel was shot to death.' I had seen a marble statue of this nurse in London.

There is a small drain-like river that flows beneath the city streets here. However, from above, no one would have been able to swear to its presence. Our hotel was called Splendid Hotel. Wherever we went, we would always leave our shoes outside the door before we went to bed. The hotel maid would brush them clean and leave them back there. When we did the same thing here, we found the shoes missing next morning! Mrs Sen came out from the adjoining room and complained that her shoes had also disappeared. At first we thought that they might have taken the shoes just then, and so we would no doubt find them later. But even after some time when the shoes did not arrive, we pressed the bell to summon the maid. The problem was that we did not know enough German to explain the whole thing to her. We hardly knew German—at the most I could say 'sehr träge' (meaning very lazy). But, if I said only this she would think that I was out of my mind. In the end, we communicated in sign language by pointing out her shoes and our bare feet. The maid smiled and to our surprise brought out the shoes from a small cabinet on the wall. We were perplexed how she could come in and place the shoes there when the door was locked at night. Going outside we saw small cabinets on the wall beside each door that could be accessed both from the outside as well as inside. The maid would service the shoes from outside and we could access them from inside. It was only then that we understood the reason for not finding our shoes.

The policemen in Brussels were very active. Those who controlled the traffic stood on raised platforms built for them at street intersections. They stood there, kept watch and controlled the traffic very efficiently.

Today is Monday, 29th of August. Leaving Brussels at 7.30 in the morning we took the train for Cologne. Just before the train departed, Mr Sen felt thirsty and I poured him some water from the gallon-jar that we were carrying with us. While we also started drinking, the two Belgian porters carrying our luggage started to warn us about something through words and gestures. We did not realise it at first but they were adamant. Pointing to an empty glass they made gestures asking us to drink up all the water. Sometimes they made strange faces and shouted, 'Customs, customs.' We then understood that they mistook our water jar as containing some alcoholic substance and were asking us to drink everything up before the customs officers confiscated it. This was why they were making such efforts and as foreigners their concern was really appreciable.

We have seen many fellow passengers buy lunch baskets at various stations. In a big, white, thick paper bag there was a bottle of red wine, a bunch of grapes or any other fruit, two buns, three or four pieces of boiled ham, a paper napkin and a paper plate. This is what is called a lunch-basket—in almost every continent, we have seen people buy such a basket and finish their lunch while travelling in a train. At noon, we reached the German city of Cologne. After settling down at the hotel and freshening up, the four of us left around 2.30 p.m. for sightseeing in the city. River Rhine was beautiful to look at and the Cologne Cathedral was worth the visit. We were told that much of the coloured glass from the decorations inside this cathedral had been removed for safe-keeping during the last World War. There were also signs of bombs being dropped from aeroplanes during that time. After a visit to the university here we went to see an eau-de-cologne factory, something the city was famous for. The manager informed us of the process of manufacturing eau-de-cologne. Fragrant flowers collected from Greece and Italy were mixed with spirit and water and then stored in vacuum tight wooden caskets. Six months later the liquid was extracted through the built-in taps of these caskets and then refined with other medicines. The process of making this eau-de-cologne was usually not disclosed to the public and we were just given a summary of the entire process. Mrs Sen and I received two eau-de-cologne bottles as gifts.

In Cologne there is a big park with several small hills within it. These are not natural but man-made—done by the German government to support jobless people after the war. We also have so many unemployed people in our country. But I would not know if there is provision to make them work under such daily labour schemes or not.

After breakfast next morning, on the 30th of August, we left the hotel at 8.30 a.m. and went to the bank of the Rhine. We had planned to go from here to Maine by steamer. With still some time left for the departure we boarded the steamer with our luggage and sat on the first floor deck. I saw people selling cart loads of peaches on the river bank. Each fruit was the size of a tennis ball and we bought some. The steamer went along for the whole day. The scenery on both sides of the Rhine was beautiful. Trains and cars ran on both sides. The vines were laden with lots of grapes. Since

Rhineland

we left India, it was for the first time that we saw in the Rhine, a real river. The mountains and the trees on either side added to the beauty. But this was nothing compared to the Ganges at Lakshman Jhola in Rishikesh. The place along the sides of the river here was known as Rhineland.

It was late in the evening by the time we reached Maine. We had finished our dinner on the steamer itself and so went to the station to board another train that took us to Frankfurt after some time. We were very tired, our eyes burdened with sleep. On reaching the hotel thus, we changed our clothes, hit the bed and slept.

Early in the morning, on the 1st of September we packed and got ready to leave for Berlin. The four of us boarded a taxi while three or four German porters carried our big suitcases along in hand-drawn pulley carts. When they took a different route, I panicked and shouted in Bengali, '*Oh Ma! Ora jey onnoe rastaye jaachchey!*' [Oh my God! They are going in a different direction!] I think one of the porters

An omnibus full of tourists in Berlin

understood my anxiety through my gestures and so he smiled and said, 'Bahnhof, bahnhof,' meaning 'we are going to the station.'

We had some time at our disposal after we packed in the morning and went out into the street to buy some bananas and peaches for our journey. It was noon by the time we boarded the train and since we had to spend the whole day in the train both Mrs Sen and I engaged ourselves in knitting. It was late at night when we reached Berlin and the hotel we stayed was called Christl. Hospiz St. Michael.

On the morning of 2nd September we took a tour by motorbus, spent the whole day visiting different parts of the city, and then hit the road for Potsdam which was the summer residence of the German emperor Kaizer. The garden house with its fountain was very beautiful. We took the bus and reached the bank of River Havell a little further away. Here we disembarked from the bus and boarded a motor launch. We had our lunch on board the launch. A little later we got down and boarded another bus which drove along the river and beautiful gardens. In one garden we saw some marble statues of men and women standing in a circle and holding hands. They were all nude but different kinds of creepers surrounded their bodies. Some had different flowers blooming too. At first glance it seemed that the statues were wearing green clothes with floral prints on them. This was known as the Orangery.

The palace gardens were also beautiful, as if cut out step by step on the mountain slope. Also, the bedroom, the music room and the coral room of the palace were worth seeing. The roof or ceiling of the coral room was adorned with oceanic animals like crocodiles, sharks, etc. The scales on the bodies of these sculptures were done up with real shells. The walls of the rooms were decorated with precious stones like amethysts, rubies, emeralds, pearls, etc. The Kaizer had received all these precious stones from different countries as gifts. Before entering the palace a special pair of heavy shoes had to be worn over one's own shoes because the floor was too polished and thus slippery. These shoes prevented one from slipping or falling down. All the artifacts belonged to the Kaizer before the war. Plays would be performed inside the palace where there was a stage and a gallery for the audience. After seeing all this, when I was proceeding towards the bus, the police called me to point out that I was still wearing those special shoes. Everyone started to laugh when I went to return them. The Berlin Zoo was also very neat and clean. Besides the aquarium, there were many seals here. During our stay in Berlin we also noticed that beautifully decorated plants with blooming flowers were placed on the windowsills of each house. If we tried to decorate plants in this manner in our country, they would either be destroyed during the storms or at least half of them would be devoured by sparrows even before that.

On the morning of 3rd September we left Berlin for Vienna. Since the distance was considerable, we decided to stop for the night at Prague, the capital of Czechoslovakia instead of spending it in the train. We reached Prague at 1.30 p.m. and stayed there for two nights. This city was also the home of the famous Bata shoe company. Though we had visited all the important places here, I cannot recollect them very well now.

We left Prague on the morning of the 5th of September and reached Vienna, the capital of Austria, around four in the afternoon. Mr and Mrs Sen parted from us at the station and since we had planned to stay in Vienna for a while, we went to a cheaper accommodation. Our hotel was called Hospiz Rosauernante and being informed of our arrival beforehand, the owner herself came to receive us at the station. She escorted us to her hotel, showed us our room

The Clock Tower in Prague

and introduced us to her secretary who would look after us during her absence. She could not speak English well, but understood everything. The lady secretary was also very pleasant. She had a lean, tall figure and was always in a jovial mood. The thought of keeping us happy always kept her busy.

Before leaving Calcutta, my father had written a letter of introduction to Professor Sigmund Freud, the famous psychologist, and had instructed us to meet him if we ever visited Vienna. He would be able to help us in many ways. As he no longer lived in the address furnished in our introductory letter, the proprietress of our hotel helped us in locating Professor Freud. It was summer and he was living in his summer residence during this time. We got hold of this new address but were informed that except for very urgent matters, Professor Freud did not meet outsiders. I then requested the secretary to cxplain to him that we had come from Calcutta with a letter of reference from Dr Bose. After this we were informed that Professor Freud had agreed to meet us and had also allotted a fixed time for the appointment. In due course we took the street directions and tram route from the secretary and began our search for Mr Freud. On the way we saw a small shop at the corner of the street selling ripe cucumber, sweet lime and a few other fruits. The old shopkeeper was cleaning the store front with a long broom. He gaped at us in wonder—struck at seeing a sari-clad woman perhaps! I asked him the direction to Professor Freud's house. In the first instance he did not understand what I was saying; on repeating the question again he came forward with a smile and said, 'Yah, yah, Professor Freud' and pointed to one direction of the street. Walking down that way we came to an old garden house and on cross-checking the address we understood that Professor Freud lived here. There was no name on the door.

Sigmund Freud

The maid of the house was cleaning the garden path and she stared at us in wonder. We asked her to inform Professor Freud that we had come to meet him. She did not understand anything because she didn't know English but on hearing the words 'Professor Freud' assumed that we had come to meet him. She then gave us a smile and said, 'Bitteschön'. We would hear this word quite frequently during our stay here. In the morning as soon as we sat down at the breakfast table, the maid would utter 'Bitteschön'. Later, when we wanted to go out, she would hurriedly open the door and say 'Bitteschön' once again. At night before going to bed, before shutting the door, the maid would again say 'Bitteschön'. I often wondered what this word meant and later came to know that it was somewhat like the English word 'please'.

When we pressed the doorbell, another maid opened the door and ushered us inside the house. On entering we saw different pictures hanging just below the staircase. Some tables and chairs were laid out in such a manner that they served the purpose of a lounge. I was surprised to see that such a renowned psychologist had such meagre arrangements. People in these countries lived in such sparse settings. All their showing off is when they visit a poor country like ours. On seeing the Buckingham Palace from outside in London I had realised that our Governor's House and the Mullick Palace at Chorbagan were much larger.

Professor Freud came out of a room after a few minutes and greeted us. Reading about him in newspapers and journals I had imagined this world-famous psychologist to be someone very impressive in appearance. Instead he turned out to be an old, shaky and ordinary-looking man, who held a burning cigar in his hand and whose teeth were all framed in gold. He came forward and asked me, 'Are you Dr Bose's daughter? I am acquainted with your father through correspondence but have never met him personally. Now I am seeing you before seeing him. What does he look like? When will he come to Vienna? How is he?' he asked.

After that he took us for a stroll in his garden. Both the house and the garden were very old. Freud told us that the house did not belong to him. The owner of the house was once a wealthy man but had now fallen upon hard times. There were many apple trees in the garden. Freud introduced us to his wife and sister-in-law. They did not speak English but understood it. His daughter Miss Anna Freud was at that time attending the Psychoanalytic Congress at Wiesbaden. We heard that she knew English well and also acted as a secretary to her father. After the stroll in the garden we went back inside the room. Two huge furry dogs ran in. One jumped onto Freud's lap and the other put his front paws up on my lap and tried to climb up. I was stiff with fear. I was not in the habit of living with dogs but just kept quiet for courtesy's sake. Picking up an ivory statue of Lord Vishnu from his table, Freud said, 'Your father had once sent it to me.' The dog suddenly gave a loud bark and jumped up on to my lap. At that moment, I too forgot all courtesy, pushed him out of my lap and stood up from the chair. Dogs in these countries were used to getting hugs from visitors, so why would he listen to me? Considering me a spoilsport, he started barking even louder. Freud understood my situation and quickly took the two dogs to another room and locked them up. They went on barking loudly and banged on the door.

'Are you afraid of dogs?' Professor Freud asked me.

'Yes, I do not have dogs. I am very scared of them.'

'Why are you scared? I make the dogs sit on my lap and feed them. Your father treats other people's mental diseases. Does he know about your fear of dogs?'

'Yes, of course he knows,' I replied. 'He himself does not like dogs. He too does not have any dogs.'

Freud was surprised to hear this.

I kept on thinking. If I could speak fluent English, I would ask Professor Freud at least once what his own love of dogs signified. Being a famous psychologist, what did he think about it?

We had heard that Vienna was famous for its doctors and good medical treatment and we needed to consult a good doctor. On asking Freud about it, he recommended the name of Dr Felix Doyce. Dr Doyce asked us to go and live for a few days at Porto Rosso near Trieste in Italy. Most of the gentlemen in Vienna were either doctors or professors by profession.

Six

We stayed in Vienna for five days and saw whatever was worth seeing. Special mention has to be made of Schönbrunn, the palace of the erstwhile kings of Austria. The garden of this palace resembled the one at Versailles but was not that pretty. Old vehicles used by the royalty were kept inside the palace. The state-coach or the car used by the king to travel around had sixteen horses attached to it. The horses were all made of wood—their shape and stride were very beautiful. White in colour, they had red velvet harnesses and brass ornaments. The car was like an old-fashioned Brougham. All these items were displayed for the visitors in a big hall along with the clothes of the last king and queen of Austria. We also saw the bedroom, the library, the dining hall, the lounge and the picture gallery.

The Schönbrunn Palace

In Vienna we commuted by tram. We have seen trams in many places but none of them were as good as our trams in Calcutta. While travelling in a tram one day a man asked us, 'Are you from Sudan?' We told him that we were not from Sudan but from India. Though we were dark skinned, no doubt, I kept on wondering how he could compare us to the Sudanese people.

Our room in the hotel was on the sixth floor and we would access it through the lift. The canal of the Danube River could be seen from the window of our room. There was a small park at the side of the canal. Each day around noon, scantily clothed people, both young and old, would come and sunbathe in this park. The sight was very awkward for us to see but people here were so conscious of preserving their health that they did not feel ashamed about it. There was a cake shop nearby from which we would often buy cakes. We would also buy good peaches frequently, from the woman selling them at the crossing on the other side of the street.

One day, we got lost in the street. We asked a man which tram to board so that we could go back to our hotel. Identifying us as foreigners, he asked, 'Are you new to the place? Don't you know anything here?' Instead of taking a tram he asked us to take the underground train so that we could reach our hotel easily. We requested him to show us the way. He then accompanied us and also boarded the underground train as he had a monthly pass for it. When the train stopped, we climbed up and saw that we had reached the same park next to the Danube canal. We were unaware of such an easy method of commuting near our hotel and it really eased our journey. This attitude of helping out foreigners is something that I must especially make mention of.

A couple of days before leaving Vienna, Miss Freud came back from Wiesbaden and invited both of us for lunch. She called and said that she would pick us up in her car. On the scheduled day we went along with her and reached the house of her doctor friend Ruth Brunswick. Miss Anna Freud told us that since it was a little inconvenient to play host to us at her own house, she had arranged this lunch at her friend's place. The doctor friend was also a psychiatrist, a disciple of Professor Freud. She practiced medicine but her husband was a music teacher who played the piano. They also had a daughter—a small and sweet child!

After lunch, Miss Freud and Ruth Brunswick sat down to chat with me. Among the different topics of discussion, the most important one was the sari worn by Indian women. I was wearing a deep blue *zari*-bordered sari and both of them liked it very much. Miss Freud wanted to know how I wore the sari after the tailor stitched it for me. Did I put it over my head or pull it up from the feet? I told her that our saris were not made by tailors and we wear it ourselves. Ruth then wanted to know how long a sari was. When she heard that it was six yards long, she further asked, 'How can you manage this long piece of cloth without the help of a tailor?' Miss Freud then asked, 'Do you always wear this dress?' I told her that this was a formally draped sari but at home we wore saris of much simpler designs, in another way. Both of them then requested me to show them the two different methods of wearing saris and politely added that if I could show them and did not mind doing it, it would make them very happy indeed. I agreed and the two friends quickly shut all the doors and windows so that I could demonstrate. They were very pleased and thanked me enormously. After a while, Miss Freud left for some work; Ruth's husband too now sat on the piano. In the meantime, Ruth took me in her car for a drive outside Vienna to show me the countryside.

We took leave of the Brunswick couple after Miss Freud returned and she dropped us back to our hotel.

I had seen people in London using their own spit for certain specific jobs and saw the same thing being repeated in Vienna too. The lady secretary of our hotel would stick postage stamps on the envelope with spit. One day I went with her to post some books to my father in India. She said that the expensive stamps were exhausted and so I had to stick eight inexpensive ones on the book packet. When I agreed, she took out eight stamps and started to lick them quickly. At first I kept quiet, but after the fifth stamp was pasted, I could no longer control myself. I asked her why she did not keep a bowl of water to do the job. She had probably never heard such a question before and feeling a little embarrassed said that the servants had forgotten to keep it. I told her to ask for water immediately and to never do it again as it was a very bad habit. For the rest of my stay at that hotel in Vienna, I saw a bowl of water always kept on the table.

I had a bad toothache one day and visited Dr Felix Doyce to have it attended. He asked me to press the gums with one finger for some time. After the examination was over, I asked for some water to wash my hands. He hurriedly paced from one corner of the room to the other and said, 'Well, I don't have water. It's very difficult to get it. I'll clean your hand in another way.' Saying this he dabbed some spirit on cotton wool and wiped my fingers. It was quite surprising that there was no provision of water in a doctor's chamber. So it was hardly a surprise that ordinary people would be miserly about it.

Before leaving Vienna we went to meet Professor Freud again. We thanked him a lot and bid him farewell. We were foreigners who knew nothing of Vienna. We shall always remember the attention and hospitality that we received from Professor Sigmund Freud, Miss Anna Freud, Dr Brunswick and others. The memory shall always remain in our hearts. Things would not have been so comfortable without their help.

It was quite warm in Vienna during this time and woollen clothes were not required. Whenever I went out, I would always wear my overcoat otherwise people would go on staring at my sari in an odd manner. If I stopped for a while, literally a crowd would gather around me. The cover of the coat helped me a lot. I heard that Vienna was very cold in winter.

On the morning of 11th September we left Vienna for Italy. The train went through the Austrian Alps, sometimes going through tunnels. All the tunnels were not dark. In some the stone columns and arches were constructed in such a manner that it seemed that the train was passing through a pillared hallway. Along our route, a sandy river accompanied us. There was very little water in it and those little bits were blue in colour. It seemed to be snowing on the mountains but in reality it was not so. There was no snow on the peaks, just rocks and sand, but the rays of the sun reflecting upon them created such an illusion.

On the train we met a Japanese gentleman who knew English. Mahatma Gandhi was in jail during that time and he asked us about it saying, 'It was very wrong to imprison him in such a way. We don't like the English, they cheat people a lot.' We also got acquainted with an Italian couple who were going to Trieste. They knew very little English. When we told them that we would go to Venice and then to Porto Rosso, the man suggested that we should not take such a long route. He adviced us to get down at Trieste, stay in some hotel near the station and leave the next morning by steamer ferry for a two-hour ride across the Adriatic Sea and reach Porto Rosso. We agreed to his proposal and got off at Trieste.

Trieste is located on the Adriatic Sea. The water of the sea was deep blue in colour and without any waves looked as calm as a lake. The harbour at Trieste looked magnificent by moonlight. Big Italian ships belonging to the Lloyd Tristino Company all departed from here. We stayed at a hotel where the proprietress arranged a room for us. Dinner time was already over, so we had to survive on tea, bread, butter and jam. After breakfast next morning, there was still some time left to go to the harbour and so we sat down to chat with the lady. After several other topics our conversation again went back to Gandhi. The proprietress said, 'Gandhi has asked you to use swadeshi products and stop buying foreign goods. So what harm has the British government done in imprisoning him and his followers? It is a good deed and everyone wants the development of his own nation. What harm is it causing to your government?'

We told her that for every sterling pound in Britain (i.e., 20 shillings), five shillings was earned from India. If we boycott foreign goods then these five shillings are lost. The government has to look for its own advantages and hence it had to make such arrangements. Hearing this, the lady said, 'I understand. Mahatma Gandhi does not belong to our country but we always worship him in our minds.'

The bus that was to take us to the ferry harbour arrived after some time and we boarded it along with our luggage. Before the ship left, I bought some peanuts for one lira from a man selling them on the shore. We started chatting with the captain once the ship left. After working in different ships he had now settled on this job of Trieste-Porto Rosso ferry service. The two-hour distance between Trieste and Porto Rosso could be covered by an airplane in five minutes and we saw two or three planes making such trips.On

Trieste: Plane heading for Porto Rosso

reaching Porto Rosso, we walked to our hotel called Pension Helio.

This place is located on the sea coast and is surrounded by hills and a few islands. When we reached the reception, the hotel owner was not there so we went out to the adjoining garden. Here we found people sitting on chairs or lying down on the sand basking in the sun. There were more women than men and all of them had skimpy bikinis on—nearly half naked you could say. A lady walked up to us. She was German and conveyed in broken English that the manager had gone to Trieste on some errand and would return only in the evening and that she could help us. We told her we needed a good room because we wanted to stay here for a few days. She arranged a small sea-facing room on the first floor. Since people here bathe in the sea, there was only one common toilet and no private bathrooms in the entire hotel. The flush in the toilet didn't work and I failed to understand how so many people lived here. Hungry and exhausted, we didn't bother much and instead went downstairs to eat.

No one knew English here so we could not tell the waitress who came to serve us what we wanted to eat. After a lot of effort, and with the help of that German lady, we told her that we did not eat beef and so needed boiled eggs and fried potatoes. The day passed by but at night when we were attacked by hordes of mosquitoes, we decided that we would leave this place early in the morning. We were unable to bear both water shortage and sleep deficiency.

Early next morning we went searching for a better hotel and found one called 'Palace Hotel'. We spoke to the manager who said that there was wire meshing in the windows to prevent mosquitoes. We came back and when we informed the manager that we were leaving his hotel he was unhappy. He said that since we did not eat beef, he had spent a lot of money procuring chickens for us and we had to pay for that before leaving. This made him happy and he gave us a few big peaches and said, 'Taste them. Palace Hotel does not serve such good ones.'

We felt relieved in the Palace Hotel. There were no mosquitoes disturbing us, the taps had running water and the toilets were clean. There were plenty of red, black and white grapes at Porto Rosso; peaches were also very cheap. There were many shops selling different kinds of bathing costumes and other gadgets. There were photo shops also. We would stand in our balcony and watch the planes departing from the airport here to Trieste. They would run on a slope and touch the Adriatic Sea, then after spraying water like a fountain, would gradually take off. People would spend the whole day sun bathing and then bathe in the sea.

One day we boarded a tram and went to a far off place called Pirano. It was an ancient town. That German lady accompanied us and she told us that this place was originally a pirate den but had now turned into a fisherman's enclave. We walked on the sand and saw several fishing boats and nets drying. The entire place had a stinking smell. There was an old fort on top of a small hill. The sun was setting and the still blue water of the Adriatic Sea looked very beautiful. The small hilly islands surrounding us were filled with vineyards that came down right up to the seashore.

It is worth watching the Italian police who always move around in pairs. They were very particular about their dress which was shiny black with silver and golden buttons. The tilted cap on the head had feathers of different colours stuck on it. With an indelible smile on their lips, their looks were somewhat secretive. The gait was leisurely. Altogether, from their appearance and their attitude they looked more like dolls to be preserved in glass cases rather than real policemen! Across the hotel there was a garden with strong fencing and paved steps that led to the sea. We would go there every evening to bathe in the sea. During our stay in Porto Rosso, we had befriended an old French gentleman who spoke English with great difficulty. He would often chat with us and whenever he talked about his wife, he would refer to her as 'my woman'.

After staying for nine days at Porto Rosso we went back to Trieste and then on to Venice. We left Trieste by car on the afternoon of the 21st of September and reached Venice the same evening. Venice is also situated on the shore of the Adriatic Sea. The Italians call Venice, Venezia. The streets of Venice are full of canals and they were like narrow rivers. There was the Grand Canal from which several other narrow canals branched off like lanes from the main street. The water was blue in colour but since the Italians are very dirty they dropped household garbage—dust and dirt collected after brooming, torn pieces of paper and shreds of cloth, dirty water left over after mopping the floors, spit, skins peeled off vegetables—from their windows straight into this water. The houses on either side of the canals did not seem to be either clean or fashionable. There were some flowering creepers on the balconies but next to them were kept rusty tin boxes, broken baskets, torn clothes, etc. Even tiny mice swam in these waters. Just as they did in our country, here too people did not hesitate to urinate on the streets. The street urchins played hide and seek, twisted tops and indulged in occasional fights. We had not noticed such things in the other countries we visited.

Just as trams and buses ply on bigger roads and taxis and horse-drawn carriages in the smaller ones back in our country, here there were steamer and motor boat services on the Grand Canal. Daily, weekly, and monthly tickets were available for these rides. There were gondolas in the narrow canals. These boats assembled in their termini just as horse carriages or rickshaws do. The boatmen would shout, 'Gondola, gondola' to attract people whenever they saw them walking along the paved streets on both sides of the canal. People usually used the overbridge when they needed to commute between houses or go to the opposite side of the road. Among the many overbridges, the Rialto Bridge was the most important and it has even been mentioned in Shakespeare's *The Merchant of Venice.* Since it took a longer time to commute to different places using the pavements or streets, people usually preferred the waterways.

The largest crossing here is known as Piazza San Marco. In Italy, squares are known as piazzas. Several big shops, the Dodge's Palace, the office of Lloyd Tristino Company, and many others are all located at San Marco. Italy is famous for its music, painting, sculpture and art. Concert parties assemble on the pavements in front of these big shops and entertain the pedestrians and audiences alike. Each shop has its own individual set of musicians. Chairs and tables are laid out in front of the shops and people can have tea, soda or ice-cream while listening to these musical performances. In just one day I realised that the Italians were very fond of music.

While having dinner at the hotel we heard brisk footsteps of hundreds of people on the street. On enquiring the hotel boy told us that people had been busy all this while listening to the music at San Marco and after the shops closed down at 8 p.m., they were now returning home. When I pass through Mirzapur Street in Kolkata and see many people standing on the pavement in front of the sweet shops listening to the radio, I am always reminded of San Marco. Of course it is needless to say that the quality of music at San Marco was excellent. Necklaces made of glass beads, different kinds of lampshades, tea sets with golden design, flower vases and many other things were manufactured in Venice. Venetian lace was also very pretty. The two islands of Murano and Burano in the Adriatic Sea have schools for teaching lace making and factories for producing different kinds of glass objects. Beautifully embroidered Spanish shawls were also available here. I have seen women sit in their shops and embroider these shawls very deftly. Venice is also famous for different kinds of leather goods and artifacts made from Italian marble. On reaching our hotel in Venice a man informed us of an exhibition of Venetian glass being held nearby. We walked to that place after dinner. Beautiful objects made of marble, alabaster and glass were displayed in such a manner that one wished one could stand and look at them for a long time.

At night we could not sleep at Hotel Universo due to mosquito menace. The water on the streets was a den for mosquitoes. Fearing an attack of malaria we woke up in the morning and had five grains of quinine each. Since we had to come back to Venice to board our ship back to India, we went out looking for a better hotel where there would be no mosquitoes. It was called Hotel Manilo Pilsen.

One day we took a gondola to visit a shop on the Grand Canal. It was called Salviatti and the glass items manufactured here were worth looking at. A big glass vessel was put in an oven. Artisans used long iron pipes, lifted the liquid glass and blew through the other side of the pipe to make different designs of flowers, leaves, human figures, etc. It is not easy to describe this process unless one sees it with one's own eyes. I saw a beautiful bunch of grapes made of glass. Glass vines entwined the huge columns and the leaves were made of different shades of green glass. The grapes were light green, red and purple in colour. There were electric bulbs lit inside these bunches of grapes.

One day we went to visit the Dodge Palace situated next to the San Marco Piazza. The dodges were similar to the dukes in England. With a dungeon beneath it, the palace looked quite old. Guards were posted beside each door. Different kinds of pigeons built their nests here. Feeding these pigeons each evening at San Marco was a grand affair.

Venice has innumerable lanes and by-lanes. These can be compared to the famous lanes of Kashi (Benaras). One day, while coming out of a leather goods shop in San Marco, I noticed a lady clad in a sari. Her husband was also with her. They saw us and came forward to introduce themselves. The gentleman was a Mr Latif. They lived in Hyderabad and were returning from a tour of Europe. He was an excellent man. With the two of them we formed a group and went to visit Rome and Florence. We saw several churches there and the marble work inside them was very beautiful.

We stayed here for two nights. One evening when we sat down for dinner, I suddenly noticed an Italian lady calling me. At first I thought that I had fallen victim to another uncivilised woman and there were reasons behind this belief. There have been several instances in the streets of Italy when women called me and when I went closer, they made uncouth gestures with their hands. But this lady was not of that kind. Later I came to know that both she and her husband were good violin players. At one time an Italian concert troupe had gone to Calcutta and these two had also toured India. From my sari she had recognised me as an Indian lady and asked me, 'Why haven't you applied the red dot on your forehead? People in your country chew a kind of leaf after their meals that turn their lips red. Don't you eat those leaves?' I told them that those leaves were called *paan* and that one could not carry these with oneself for long. After some conversation, her husband said, 'What do you want to drink? Have some champagne with us.' We told them that we did not have champagne. 'Then shall I ask for some whiskey?' On hearing that we did not even have that, he added, 'Then have some sherry.' When we refused sherry, port, beer, or any drink he asked in a frustrated tone, 'Don't you drink any of them? How do you live without drinking? Don't you feel thirsty?' We said that we were satisfied with water when we were thirsty. In the end we pacified them by having a glass of lemonade.

At 11 o'clock on the 22nd of September, the four of us left for Florence and reached there at five in the afternoon. We stayed in a boarding house looked after by an aged German lady. With an ever-smiling face, her behaviour was very polite. For the three days that we stayed here, her hospitality made us forget that we were on foreign land. She also treated the poor women who worked here as maids like her own daughters. I noticed that after serving us lunch she would eat at the same table along with these maids. I saw that she even helped them in the kitchen.

We visited a mosaic factory where different floral and scenic designs were created by using small stones of various colours. Situated by the Arno River, Florence was famous for its mosaic and was also the birthplace of the Italian poet Dante. There were several bridges across the Arno and along the oldest bridge were shops on both sides selling gold and silver jewellery, different kinds of stone and leather goods. One day we went to visit the Uffizi and Pitti Galleries that had the paintings of famous painters like Michelangelo, Raphael and Murilo. There were also very beautiful marble sculptures.

Whenever we went out, people gathered around us on the streets calling us 'Indiano'. One day, a man saw Mrs Latif and me standing on the street and suddenly came forward, clicked a picture and disappeared. He didn't even bother to seek our permission. Everybody here including coolies, porters, drivers, and newspaper sellers were out to fleece foreigners like us. One day we went out to buy a newspaper and asked the shopkeeper whether he had change. He said, 'Yes' but after taking the money refused to return the change. Most of our exchanges took place either through gestures or with the help of a dictionary. In Italy, people did not understand any foreign language except French. We returned the newspaper to him and said that we did not want it and asked him to refund the full amount. He then smiled and handed us the newspaper along with the change.

Back home, Mahatma Gandhi was fasting in an Indian jail and this news was being published in different Italian newspapers. So wherever we went people would eagerly ask us questions like, 'What is the news in India? How long do you think India will take to gain her independence? When will Gandhi be released?'

9 Seven

On the 25th of September we left Florence for Rome. The train left at 9 a.m. and we reached the Italian capital at five in the afternoon. Rome is situated next to River Tiber. We stayed in a boarding house run by a Christian sect. As there was no one else except an old servant called Bruno, all the work here was done by some 'sisters'. Bruno acted as the sweeper and also carried the luggage of the boarders. The sisters were very polite but they did not understand any other language except German. We found it very difficult to explain things and had either to use the dictionary or take the help of Baedeker's guide book.

The sight of Rome instantly reminds us of its history. This place is not flat but situated within four or five small hills. And so some of the streets in Rome are plain, while others are undulated, sloping up and down. The streets of Rome were cleaner and wider than those in other Italian cities. Like in our country, here also we saw horse-drawn garbage cars and sweepers cleaning the streets with brooms and pots made of tin. In all the big streets of Italy we saw the statue of Garibaldi.

Whenever we went out sightseeing, we hired a private motorcar along with an English-speaking guide from Thomas Cook & Company. They also had coaches for tourists but we would have to move around according to fixed schedules in order to avail of them. Though it was more expensive to travel on our own, we could move around when we wanted, taking our own time and this made us less tired.

The city of Rome is surrounded by a wall that in earlier times was the rampart of a fort. On this wall there were several half-lion and half-woman figures made of stone—they were sculpted beautifully. The guide informed us that the Roman emperors brought these from Egypt as part of their victory booty and installed them on the walls of the fortress. All these incidents took place before the birth of Christ but the statues did not look as old as that. There were also different kinds of fountains on the streets. It was a pleasure to see these fountains and I liked the Neptune fountain the best. The sea-god Neptune stood with the reins of eight powerful horses in his hands and his posture was excellent. Water came out incessantly from the nose and mouth of these horses. Some of these fountains were old and traditional while others were retrieved by Mussolini from different places and reinstalled.

The Vatican spread out on a large area outside the city. Part of this was turned into an Egyptian museum with mummies and other objects. The mummies kept in wooden coffins with glass cases were the most interesting to watch. Some of them were even kept in a standing position. In those times people from the genteel fashionable society loved to possess Egyptian objects made of alabaster, so there is an abundance of them everywhere in Italy. Inside the Vatican there is the palace of the Pope, adjoining gardens and a museum. It would take at least seven days to see the Vatican properly. The Pope received various kinds of books, flower vases and other items as gifts from kings of various countries. These were displayed in the museum. Some of the books had precious stones like emeralds, rubies and diamonds embossed on their covers. It was amazing to see the marble sculptures of Michelangelo. The muscles carved out on the body, the veins and the look in the eyes of the statues were perfected in such a manner that they seemed real. Besides these, his embroidery work, carpet designs and oil paintings were also worth seeing. One surface of a huge wall was full of Michelangelo's paintings and the length and height of that hall was like a small house in our country. Many churches in Rome had been built under the guidance of Michelangelo as he was a connoisseur in engineering, painting, embroidery and sculpture.

We then went to see the gymnasiums and baths of the Roman kings. These had all the necessary arrangements for keeping the body healthy, well-built and attractive. The men wrestled with stout wrestlers and there was arrangement for mud bath, ice bath, hot and cold water bath. The women on the other hand would avail of sun-bathing, bathing in clear, lukewarm water, and even bathed in milk produced by cows and donkeys. Different kinds of bathtubs and fountains used for this purpose had been partially dug out and recovered from beneath the earth. They even had oil massages before taking bath. The gymnasium was surrounded by marble statues of warriors.

Rome itself had about two hundred cathedrals and to see each of them in detail would have required us to stay longer. The largest one was St. Peter's Cathedral. The Roman emperors looted the best marble columns and products from around the world and kept them here. Expensive objects and stone statues from King Solomon's treasury were also kept here. Some stone columns or obelisks brought from Egypt and Greece also adorned the street junctions in Rome. The height of some of these columns were equal to twelve or thirteen storeyed buildings in our country but since they were carved out from one single piece of stone, they were without any joints. I do not know whether it is possible to bring such a huge piece of stone from another country now. Even if it was possible it would require a lot of brainwork to do so. But the Roman kings brought them very easily by floating them in rafts along the sea route. I had seen pictures depicting such a scene at the Pope's palace in the Vatican.

One day while roaming on the streets of Rome, Mrs Latif and I bought two bunches of night queen flowers that were much better in quality and fragrance than our home-grown counterparts. A little later Mrs Latif bought some big and bright red chillies from another shop. Returning to our hotel she cut them into small pieces, mixed some ginger, salt, mustard and onions and made a *chutney* with which we relished our bread and mashed potato meal. The same evening she went and purchased a huge watermelon and we all enjoyed eating it. These watermelons looked and tasted similar to the ones found in Goalondo in our country.

A long time ago the Romans were pagans. This meant that they were idol-worshippers like the Hindus and even cremated their friends and relatives after death. However, once Christianity spread in the country, the Christians started fearing the Pagans because they were more in number and would not allow them to bury their dead. Sometimes they even dug up the graves and burnt the dead bodies. To gain respite from the Pagans, the Christians built a temple. Ordinary people thought that it was meant for worship but in reality it was built with the coffins of the dead. The walls of this temple had innumerable dead bodies stuck on them. Each step of the staircase was made with the dead bodies of men. The last level of this temple was a dark courtyard full of small and big graves. So that the departed souls could rest in peace, one had to hold two candles, one in each hand and enter this place and leave them burning there. The air inside was stale and this was called the catacomb.

On the left side of the catacomb there was a beautiful motor road that led to Austria on the shore of the Tyrrhenian Sea. The scenery was wonderful. In ancient times, part of Rome was known as Matharan but that place is now buried in the ground. Mussolini is now digging up this place and several things are being excavated—the court, houses, roads, the Temple of Jupiter, stone figures of Venus, various kinds of dolls, beautiful railings and columns, etc. Though it resembled the ruins of Pompeii, it was also significantly different. The excavated items are being reused—even broken statues of stone are being used to construct new buildings. Grand and ornate entry gates have been unearthed too. While some of them date back to the time of the Roman Emperor Nero, some could be traced to the times of Julius Caesar, that is, much before the birth of Christ. I heard that Julius Caesar built some of these arches after he returned victorious from different wars and he would enter his capital Rome through them. Latin, which was the commonly used language at the time, was used in the inscriptions on the head of the doors and the walls. S.P.Q.R. meaning Senatus Populus Que-Romanus (Senate of the Roman People) indicated the Legislative Assembly.

After this we went to see the famous Colosseum in Rome, though I cannot remember now who built it. On the way we saw a huge pile of bricks and stone that were remnants of the palace of King Nero. The Colosseum was a huge affair and can be called a city in itself. It resembled a circular house about four or five storeys high. There were stairs leading to each floor but fearing damage stepping on them was prohibited. Once upon a time there were shops and hotels inside the Colosseum and the emperors of Rome and other affluent people would enjoy themselves here. There were seating galleries almost one storey high in the circular open space at the center. The outside wall and columns had beautiful stone sculptures of women, warriors, and the Greek god Apollo. After these got destroyed, Mussolini moved them elsewhere. The circular courtyard was the site for dance performances by beautiful women, duels between warriors, sword fighting and different kinds of fights between men and fierce animals. The preparations for the fight between men and wild beasts would begin days ahead. The wild animals would be kept starving for seven or eight days in a room in the Colosseum and then released on the day scheduled for the fight. Prior to their release runaway slaves, prisoners, and sometimes strong men would be kept standing in the centre of the arena. When the starved beasts would pounce on them, then some of them would die, some instantly, others giving up after a chivalrous fight. Occasionally however, a few of them triumphed. Warriors and kings, the rich and the noble, even the aristocratic ladies, would sit and enjoy such a cruel entertainment. This kind of amusement continued throughout the day and food and drinks were supplied at random so that no one felt exhausted. All that I have written about the Roman Colosseum, the forum and the catacomb was from the information I garnered from the guides. Of course I had heard stories about the Colosseum earlier.

Mr and Mrs Latif stayed in Rome for only two days and then left for Naples. We had more time to spare and so we stayed here for five days. During this period one day we went to the office of Thomas Cook and Company to receive our letters. At the time, we read in the newspapers that Mahatma Gandhi had broken his fast by drinking lime juice. The Italian people were also busy discussing this newspaper report.

We had met a young Bengali man in Rome called Srijukto[1] Dhirendra Nath Das who was training as an airline pilot. From London we had sent our schedule to another Bengali man to come and meet us in Rome. For some reason he was unable to receive us and sent this young man instead. Mr Das wanted

[1] Just like adding the prefix 'Sreemati' to her own name, it is interesting that Durgabati adds the prefix 'Srijukto' to this particular Bengali name. Apart from just writing 'Mr', which essentially means a male person, which she did in the earlier paragraph when she mentions Mr and Mrs Latif, the word carries with it a sort of middle-class respectability, something pertaining to the Bengali *bhadralok* culture. Interestingly she also adds the same prefix to another Bengali gentleman's name, Jatindranath Basu.

to take us to his boarding house right from the station. Since we had already made arrangements to stay elsewhere along with the Latifs, we could not go then. Two days later Dhiren babu came to meet us at our German Home and we went to visit the Vatican with him for the second time. The same evening he invited us to his boarding house for tea.

Dhiren babu's landlady kept on staring at me for a long time. I could not understand the reason then but later she confessed that she believed Indians were much darker than us. She offered us tea and biscuits. Dhiren babu called her *Boudi* and her husband, *Dada.* The Italian 'boudi' said, 'My *thakurpo*[2] is a good man.' I told Dhiren babu that however much you taught her, she could not pronounce *thakurpo* correctly and said *thakurpe* instead. He replied that she had deliberately changed the pronunciation as that was how it was pluralised in the Italian language.

'There are five or six *thakurpos* here,' he added.

The landlady spoke more Bengali words.

'I call my husband *Ogo* and sometimes *Ogo priyo.* Do you also say *ogo*?'

My husband was amused by this question and said, 'In our country older women usually call their husbands *ogo.* Younger women address their husbands differently.'

After tea, the landlady proposed to take us for a drive in her car and we agreed. Dhiren babu would invite all Bengalis he met in Rome to his house. He showed me photographs of Srijukto Jatindranath Basu who also came to that house. After the long drive, we returned to our German Home in a tram. During our stay here we noticed something new. At night before going to bed the sister who looked after our boarding and food handed us a matchbox and a small candle

[2] In Bengali the elder sister-in-law or *boudi* always addressed the younger brother-in-law not by his name but called him *thakurpo,* meaning son of the sire, the grand patriarch.

and said, 'No light, bombard.' She could not speak any more English words than this and though she tried to explain repeatedly something in German, we could not understand it. There was a German lady-boarder in the room adjacent to ours and she could speak a little English. With her help we got to know that beginning from that night for the next three days there would be air raid practice in Rome. For this reason there would be a lot of airplanes in the sky and they would also drop artificial bombs. As per the directions of His Highness Mussolini, no one was supposed to light lamps in their rooms or go out on the streets. Anyone disobeying these orders would be fined two hundred and fifty liras or fifty rupees. About five minutes before the bombardment began, a siren would alert the citizens. Another siren would also signal the end of the exercise. We heard everything and went to bed. The sister fitted thick black curtains onto our windows in order to prevent the light from being seen out of our room.

Lying down in bed I kept on wondering when the bombardment would begin. All of a sudden there was a sharp sound of the siren and immediately the police started patrolling the streets on their motorbikes. Within five minutes the whole city fell in a slumber and immediately after that sounds of the bombardment from the sky could be heard. We were very excited and got up from bed to peer through the windows and witness this interesting event. The whole city was pitch dark and nothing was visible. Occasionally we could see the light from these artificial bombs and hear the roaring sound of the airplanes. This continued for the whole night and we went back to bed.

When we woke up in the morning, everything seemed normal and people were just walking about in the streets. We were told that the bombardment would begin again after four in the afternoon. After lunch we went for a walk on the street and on our way back the siren started sounding again.

Traffic stood still in the middle of the street and people ran to find shelter somewhere. We accompanied a group of people and entered a shop. We had been misinformed—the bombardment was to end at 4 p.m. and it was two o'clock now. So we had to remain imprisoned in that shop for two hours. When I narrated this incident to Sri Dhirendra Nath Das and he added that if any one of these artificial bombs landed on the terrace of some building, then irrespective of whether anyone was injured or not, the police would come and carry everyone to the hospital in an ambulance and admit them there. Thus all the rules that would be used during a real war were implemented in this mock attack.

We hired a phaeton one afternoon and went out. All these cars in Rome had cab meters and payment was made to the driver accordingly. But while we looked here and there we noticed that the driver suddenly turned the knob on the meter to increase the fare. He probably assumed that we did not observe his foul play. We shouted at him and he tried to explain something in Italian. On reaching home we paid him the due fare but he kept on asking for more. When we opened the Baedeker guide book and showed him the rules of payment, he left quietly. Everyone in the streets would try to fleece foreigners.

We left Rome on the 30th of September and came to Naples for the second time. In the first instance we had descended from the ship *Victoria* for only two hours to visit the ruins of Pompeii. Now we wanted to see Mount Vesuvius. We also put up in a German Home here. The young bell boys took us to the seventh floor in a glass-enclosed lift. The bad odour from their bodies made me feel like vomitting. The old landlady came forward smiling but her appearance was too harsh and the smile on her face did not suit her. We told her that we wanted a good room for two days only and we did not eat beef. In reply she said, 'Well, we get very good veal here. I will give you that.' When we said that we did not have that either she said that both lamb and chicken was rarely available here. 'If you don't like beef, why don't you try the veal?' she asked. We told her that we would have no meat at all. She could give us boiled vegetables, bread and eggs and we would manage with that.

There was a small balcony attached to our room and from there we could see the street far below us. Bare-bodied children were loitering about and people threw vegetable peels and garbage right in the middle of the street. Cows, goats and other animals also roamed about freely as they did in our country. On the other side of the street there was a mountain and on its slopes were slums. There were plenty of vineyards and trees full of peaches on the terraced slopes also. The slum dwellers spent their whole day washing clothes, carrying water, beating their children, washing utensils and spreading out their laundry to dry. A young girl of about eighteen or nineteen saw me observing all these activities from the window and started shouting 'Indiano!' Instantly hordes of old and young people came out to watch the fun. The older ones pointed their fingers and said something and the younger ones made faces and indecent gestures. I moved away from the window.

I went for a stroll along the seaside in the afternoon. The sea did not have waves as we had in the sea at Puri. On my way back I found a small shop at the road junction selling sweet lime, a few bottles of fruit syrup, ripe cantaloupes and coconuts. I bought a cantaloupe and a few strips of coconut and returned to our pension. They tasted exactly the same as in our country.

I had heard about the aquarium in Naples that had an octopus and was very keen to see it. The mention of the name of octopus brings to our mind the image of a huge animal in the sea but this one was only a miniature version of the same. At first it remained shrivelled in one corner but when a small piece of fish was dropped from above, its body doubled in size, its tentacles spread out, then it clung to the fish and ate it. Soon it returned to its earlier form. I could not differentiate between its mouth and its body. While coming back from the aquarium I heard a strange voice behind me. Turning back I saw two young girls making indecent gestures at us and laughing to their hearts' content. I kept on thinking why such grown up girls were so uncouth. At their age, girls in our country would already turn housewives and rear children.

After lunch on the 1st of October, we took a car to Mount Vesuvius. Going for a few miles the car stopped at the base of the volcano from where a mountain railway would take us to the top. Thomas Cook earlier owned it but now this was the property of the Italian Government. Our tickets had been purchased in advance and we occupied two window seats. The electric train was full of other passengers and climbed upwards. Most of the passengers were Italians and here also both children and elders pointed their fingers at us calling us 'Indiano!'

We saw the landscape outside from the train compartment. The sloped mountainside was black in colour and full of orange and peach trees. The red and black vines bent low with the weight of their fruits. The guide from Thomas Cook who accompanied us explained that the lava of the Vesuvius was very suitable for cultivating oranges and grapes. So each time there was an eruption the emerging lava both helped and created loss to the country. We gradually moved upwards and the train stopped at the observatory. A man was constantly monitoring the seismographic instrument here and sending instant messages to the city office at Naples. We then boarded another train. We could now see the blue waters of the Bay of Naples down below and many spaghetti and macaroni factories. Spaghetti and macaroni are made with flour and both of them are popular food items in Italy. The train went on ascending till it stopped at a place from where everyone had to walk. It seemed as if this huge mountain had been made of coal dust. We started walking along the mountain with the Vesuvius sharply rising on our left and a deep gorge on the right. At a distance we saw the rays of the sun reflecting on the water of the Bay of Naples—the water sparkled like diamonds. The glare hurt our eyes. The path on which we walked was about five or six feet wide and at last we reached the top.

The central peak of the Vesuvius had cracked in the lava eruption of 1928 and a large crater had been created. Dark smoke continuously came out from this huge hole and it seemed as if ten or twelve coal ovens had been lit together. The smoke also changed colours—sometimes it was white, sometimes yellow, sometimes black or grey. We could inhale the smell of sulphur in it. The crater was surrounded by a circular valley that had turned hard like stone with different kinds of minerals. Most of these stones were yellowish in colour, somewhat similar to the yellow sandalwood found in Vrindavan. The soil was still soft and hot in some places and so people did not walk there. We were told that sometimes the smell of sulphur was so strong that people could not even come close. At present the Vesuvius was quiet—while we stayed there, we did not hear any sound. Local guides took the tourists right up to the mouth of the crater and a few of our fellow American tourists ventured to do just that. On our return journey the train company treated us with tea and cakes in a hotel, the price of which was included in the ticket. We came back to Naples. Just to mention here—that I shall never forget the sight of this volcano ever in my life.

Mount Vesuvius

On the 2nd of October, we left Naples and came back to Florence to the boarding house where we had stayed earlier. I told the proprietress that I wanted to cook our dinner myself and she readily agreed. Our taste buds were satiated after a long time with home cooked food. Resting for the night in Florence, the following day we took the train to Venice. Our ship back to India would leave from here. Taking a gondola we reached Hotel Mannin. Since we had to stay for some days here, we revisited some of the shops and places once again. This time we saw many Indians on the streets. All of them had arrived here after touring different places and would leave for India on the same ship *Contivarde* scheduled to sail on the 7th of October. One day we met Sri Abaninath Mitra and his wife at San Marco Square. They were staying at Hotel Universo and would also travel in the same ship. Mr Mitra's hair was ruffled, his coat unbuttoned, and the muffler around his neck was hanging carelessly. When asked why he was in such a state he answered in a reprimanding tone, 'Keep quiet. I am going home now. Why do I need to dress anymore?'

Early on the morning of the 7th of October we packed our luggage, had breakfast and checked out of the hotel. We were all very happy today. After a long trip of four months we were going to sail towards our own country. We waited anxiously to board the ship. At nine o'clock we sailed in a gondola towards the Grand Canal. The ship had arrived from Trieste and was waiting there. We alighted on the Ballard Pier and the ship was a little far away. Sitting on two suitcases we both eagerly waited for the stairs to be fixed up. About an hour later we showed our clearance pass to the sergeant and boarded the ship to find our cabin. Once we located it and entered, we found our heavy luggage that we had booked in London all in place. I started checking them. I had done a thorough check similarly on

The dining hall inside the *Contivarde*

the 13th of June on board the ship *Victoria* in Bombay and was doing the same thing again today on the 7th of October. There was a huge difference between what I felt that day and what I was feeling today. Yes, that is how it felt when one went back to where one belonged. It is really a wonderful feeling!

Standing on the deck of the ship I kept watching the different passengers come up with their luggage. All of them came one after another in gondolas. Mrs J. N. Roy arrived with her son and nephew. Abani babu and his wife came. Mr Dongre, partner of the famous medicine 'Dongre's Balamrita' came with his wife and children. We got acquainted with the wife and son of the Late Jwalaprasad from Sahjahanpur of the United Provinces. They had boarded the ship at Trieste. Around eight at night Mrs

Shankar, mother of the famous dancer Uday Shankar[3] came. There was also Miss Amala Nandy, daughter of Sri Aukshoy Kumar Nandy, the proprietor of Economy Jewellery Works.[4]

We were told that the ship would not leave till late at night. So we went down again and walked to a church nearby. The doorway was very crowded and we saw a newly wed Italian couple coming out with their friends and relatives. The bride, hardly seventeen or eighteen years old, was very good looking. The groom was older, and that too

[3] A famed Bengali artiste, Uday Shankar (1900–77) was hailed as India's first modern choreographer and dancer. The elder brother of the renowned sitarist Pandit Ravi Shankar, he was the initiator of India's modern dance traditions, a key impetus for the reclaiming or renaissance of Indian classical dance forms, a founder of cultural centers for the study of dance and other arts, and the first Indian to perform in significant venues in Europe and North America. Incorporating the delicate movements of western ballet into our traditional Indian dance, he was close to the Russian ballerina Anna Pavlova and the French dancer Simkie and spent his prime years out of India from 1931–38. His wife Amala Shankar also danced with him. His son Ananda Shankar, daughter-in-law Tanushree Shankar and daughter Mamata Shankar have all tried to keep his innovative traditions alive in their own choreography and performances.

[4] Owner of the famous jewellery shop, Economic Jewellery Works located at 200, Cornwallis Street in North Calcutta, Aukshoy Kumar Nandy was a Bengali businessman whose first visit to England took place in 1924 when he was requested by the British colonial government to participate in the British Empire Exhibition—an industrial trade fair held in London for six months from May to October of that year. Denying the sponsorship where he had to take along his craftsmen and practically show how the intricate jewellery designs were made, he decided to visit the fair at his own expenses and open a stall for selling his jewellery products. In 1929, Nandy published his travelogue *Bilat Bhraman* (Travel in Vilayet), which unlike any standard travelogue by an Indian narrating his first visit to the west by cataloguing touristy information, records his interest in more practical aspects, like visiting factories and docks and observing the ground realities of Indian students in London.

short and fat. We discussed among ourselves that probably it was this man's second marriage. Before evening we boarded the ship once again, had dinner and went to sleep. The ship started sailing in the middle of the night. While coming in the *Victoria* I could not visit the engine room of the ship because of sea sickness. Now in *Contivarde* the captain honoured our request and we went down to the engine room. Twelve boilers were burning simultaneously here and the temperature was always 110 degrees. The *Victoria* ran on motor engines but the *Contivarde* still had a traditional steam engine. The cabin passengers upstairs were travelling in comfort whereas the workers below were shovelling coal in this tremendous heat. There was provision of bringing in cold air through jute bags but in spite of that we perspired a lot here. The captain made me stand beneath one such jute bag. We had to climb down with the help of an iron ladder that was so hot that we could not hold it in our bare hands. Two crewmen bandaged our hands with thick strips of cloth. There was a big automatic door made of iron in front of the engine room that prevented water from rushing into the engine boiler in case of a shipwreck. If the sunken ship was ever recovered then the boilers would remain completely unharmed.

Before reaching Bombay I had planned to stand at the deck and watch how India looked from afar. But my wish remained unfulfilled as an attack of influenza a day before kept me bedridden. The ship was nearing Bombay but lying down in bed, I did not realise it. Hearing a local dialect after ages, '*Aur thoda aage lao*' (bring it further ahead) I saw the ship close to the harbour. We rested for two days in Bombay. After recovering a little, we boarded the train on afternoon of 21st of October and reached Howrah Station, Calcutta on the morning of the 23rd.